IFLA

International Federation of Library Associations and Institutions
Fédération Internationale des Associations de Bibliothécaires et des Bibliothèques
Internationaler Verband der bibliothekarischen Vereine und Institutionen
Международная Федерация Библиотечных Ассоциаций и Учреждений
Federación Internacional de Asociaciones de Bibliotecarios y Bibliotecas

IFLA Publications 86

Information Driven Management Concepts and Themes:

A Toolkit for Librarians

by Michael E.D. Koenig
With the assistance of Morgen MacIntosh

Section on Management and Marketing

K · G · Saur München 1998

IFLA Publications
edited by Carol Henry

Recommended catalogue entry:

Koenig, Michael E.D.:
Information driven management concepts and themes : a toolkit for librarians / by Michael E.D. Koenig. With the assistance of Morgen MacIntosh. [International Federation of Library Association and Institutions], Section on Management and Marketing. – München : Saur, 1998, VII, 73 p. 21 cm
(IFLA publications ; 86)
ISBN 3-598-21815-X

Die Deutsche Bibliothek – CIP-Einheitsaufnahme

Koenig, Michael E.D.:
Information driven management concepts and themes : a toolkit for librarians / by Michael E.D. Koenig. With the assistance of Morgen MacIntosh. [International Federation of Library Association and Institutions], Section on Management and Marketing. – München : Saur, 1998
(IFLA publications ; 86)
ISBN 3-598-21815-X

Printed on acid-free paper
The paper used in this publication meets the minimum requirements of American National Standard for Information Sciences – Permanence of Paper for Printed Library Materials, ANSI Z39.48.1984.

Printed / Bound by Strauss Offsetdruck GmbH, Mörlenbach

ISBN 3-598-21815-X
ISSN 0344-6891 (IFLA Publications)

Table of Contents

Themes are listed in reverse chronological order of appearance, most recent first. Asterisks denote the importance of the topics: Prime Importance * * *, Significant Importance * *, Marginal Importance *. The most important is unquestionably Knowledge Management.

Introduction

One of the most welcome developments in the library world of the last two decades has been the burgeoning recognition in the business community of the importance of information, information issues, and the deployment and management of information and information technology. Since we as librarians are in the business of information and the management of information, these developments are of great significance. To take advantage of the opportunities presented to us, librarians must recognize and be familiar with the specific themes and concepts that contribute the individual strands of this increased recognition by the business community.

The intent of this document is to:

- provide a familiarity with these information driven themes,
- to explain terms and concepts,
- to elucidate the vocabularies and meanings as used in the business community, and
- to point the librarian/information professional to some of the key literature sources behind each theme.

The themes, twenty-one of them, are presented in roughly the reverse chronological order (most recent first) in which they appeared in the business literature. They are presented in reverse chronological order so that the newest and trendiest, and in the case of Knowledge Management the most important, are presented first, so that the reader just dipping into the book is likely to hit paydirt promptly. A chronological sequence however would have provided more context for the reader, an easier understanding of how the themes developed, their interrelatedness, and their correlation to the continuously increasing capabilities of information technology. Indeed, the person who would like to approach this as an analysis of the development of the key information related themes in the business literature of the last two decades would do well to start at the rear and progress forward.

The themes are not all of equal importance. The author has therefore grouped them into three classes: prime importance (three stars), significant importance (two stars), and marginal importance (one star). The reader who is interested in achieving the greatest impact most rapidly from the book would be well advised to scan it, and read the three star write-ups first.

Finally, there is a section, Macro Themes, which attempts to sketch some of the larger themes which run through and integrate the central theme of Information Driven Management, and which tie together and interrelate many of the twenty-one themes.

Discussion

Despite the logical overlap between the role of the librarian and the role of information and information management in modern business, that overlap is often only poorly and inadequately perceived and understood. That lack of understanding and perception typically is true both for librarians and for business administrators and those academics and others who write on business administration.

For librarians, the problem is twofold. First, the librarian seldom has the time to adequately keep up with their own professional literature, much less the time to follow the professional literature of another discipline. Second, there is a cultural gulf. Librarianship and here one must be careful of cultural differences between countries and of the difficult dynamics of different educational systems, is a profession characterized by a high degree of self-selection and a very strong and intense professional culture. That self selection and strong sense of professional identity has considerable merit, but it also has some drawbacks, one of which might be described as a certain insularity characterizing professional culture. We often do not look outside ourselves adequately and we have a tendency to resist influences from the outside.

Compounding the difficulties of the situation is the problem of vocabulary. The library community and the business community often understand words to mean very different things. (See discussion of Knowledge Management for a particularly striking example of that phenomenon).

The problem of lack of comprehension of the commonalty is at least as severe from the business administration side. There is a general incomprehension of the fact that the librarian's role is more than custodial, that it is or should be proactive, and that it is intimately involved with information technology. Perhaps the most egregious example of this blindness is that in the "archipelago" trilogy of articles by McFarland and his colleagues at the Harvard Business School (see the articles on Managing the Archipelago), articles discussing data processing, and telecommunications are mentioned as islands in "The Archipelago of Information Services", but the company library, even across the expanse of three articles is never mentioned. To a librarian, this omission is quite incredible. To us, what comes to mind first when thinking of information services is the library, and we would hope that others would also think of it first, and if not first, at least high on the list. To overlook the library entirely strikes us as quite implausible and probably perverse, difficult to accomplish merely by oversight.

Nonetheless, while the "archipelago" example is perhaps a particularly offensive case because of the context of the articles, it is not unusual in what it reveals. It is quite common for the business community and for the academics who study and write about the business endeavor to be equally unaware of the actual and potential role of the library and the librarian in the business enterprise.

The purpose of this book then is firstly to make the librarian aware and knowledgeable, and of equal importance, to arm the librarian for the purpose of educating their administration and making them more and more knowledgeable.

To these ends the toolkit attempts not only to explain the twenty-one concepts, but also to put them in context and to explain how they evolved and what they are understood to mean in the business community.

If librarians are to use the knowledge of these concepts to leverage their role in the organization, then:

- they must be knowledgeable about the concepts and their implications regarding the library's role in harnessing these concepts
- they must understand the terms as they are used in the business context, and
- typically they must educate their administration about the potential library role implementing and harnessing these concepts, and to accomplish that,

- they must interact with their administration using the vocabulary and the contexts that their administration understandings, not the vocabulary of librarianship.

A major point to be realized (discussed at greater length and sketched schematically in the final section, Macro Themes and End Note) in that these themes do not exist independently of each other, although that point is admittedly not very obvious from the professional literature. They are to a considerable degree twenty-one different facets of the same phenomenon – the recognition of the importance of information and information management to the management of organizations in general.

In many ways, one can regard the emergence of the enthusiasm for Knowledge Management (see discussion) as an almost subliminal recognition of that integrated whole. The business literature however portrays Knowledge Management as a new phenomenon both because for many writers it is only a subliminal recognition and because it is in the interest of the writer to present Knowledge Management as new and different. The relationship between those two reasons is mutually supporting.

What the recognition of this integration lends to is that if the librarian aggressively takes advantage of the situation, then he or she can be of great value to the organization. First for the roles he or she can play in implementing some of these concepts. But perhaps even more importantly, the librarian has the potential to be the educator for the administration, the person who can see and understand these themes, their interrelationship, and their fundamental integration – their central theme of information driven management. The typical business administrator is operations oriented, not information oriented, and simply does not have the background to see the forest for the trees. Similarly, the IT manager is technology and applications oriented, not information oriented, and is similarly unlikely to see past the local trees and grasp the size of the forest. The librarian, if the cards are played well, is in the right place at the right time to have a major impact on the organization.

Priority Ranking of Topics

These themes are not all of equal importance. They can be roughly classified into three categories.

Prime Importance

- Knowledge Management and Intellectual Capital (clearly the most important single topic)
- Information Technology as Competitive Advantage
- Managing the Archipelago of Information Services
- Business Process Re-engineering
- Information System Stage Hypotheses
- Competitive Intelligence
- Data Warehousing & Data Mining
- Enterprise-wide Information Analysis
- Information Technology and Organizational Structure
- Information Technology and Productivity

Significant Importance

- Core Competencies
- Hierarchies to Markets
- Information Resource Management
- MIS & DSS and External Information
- Information Driven Marketing
- Supply Chain Management
- Enterprise Resource Planning

Marginal Importance (useful to know)

- Data Driven Systems Design
- Decision Analysis
- Minimization of Unallocated Cost
- TQM and Benchmarking

Index to Additional Business Buzzwords Discussed in this Document

Index to Additional Business Buzzwords Discussed in this Document

* *

SUPPLY CHAIN MANAGEMENT & THE VALUE CHAIN

Supply chain management is in effect the successor to Just In Time (JIT) inventory management. JIT was the concept of establishing a relationship with suppliers such that instead of the purchaser ordering and receiving materials ahead of time and then warehousing them (at considerable expense), rather the supplier delivered the needed materials "just in time". It requires an established, long term and flexible relationship between purchasers and suppliers, and to a degree it puts the purchaser at the increased mercy of the supplier, but if done well it enables flexibility, quick response, and minimal warehousing and handling costs.

One noted example of JIT is its use in the Wal-Mart chain store. Point of sale information is electronically sent in near real time to various suppliers. This places the responsibility of replenishing the store's inventory with the supplier. The advantage to Wal-Mart is simplicity and lower cost, they do not check stock or place orders, their supplier does. The advantage to the supplier is prompt information, greater lead-time in arranging for shipments and therefore more effective production planning, followed by efficient production.

What enables JIT are, as in the example above, improved telecommunications and the exchange of electronic information between purchaser and supplier. Supply chain management is simply the extension of the JIT concept to supply management in general, including one's own production and processing as well as one's relations with suppliers. The terminology "Supply Chain Management" has much to do with the popularity of Michael Porter's "value chain". Porter uses the value chain as a format or template for analyzing the operations of an organization. One is urged to asses the relative importance of the various components of the value chain to an organization's operations, and to then analyze where the application of information technology could leverage the organization's effectiveness. Figure 1 shows the components of the value chain from Research and Development to Sales and Service and below each segment illustrates it with a business sector where that component is of particular importance.

Figure 1. Value Chain Analysis

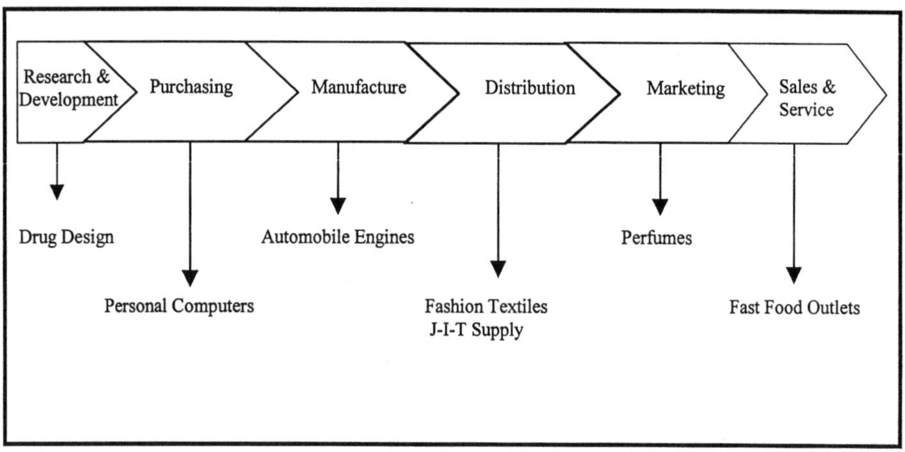

Relevance to the Librarian

While this concept generally relates to handling information that is outside the librarian's normal realm, it does have relevance to librarians in two ways. First, the notion of the value chain fundamentally derives from the argument (and assumes as a given) that all of an organization's operations are affected and can be enhanced by better use of information and information technology. This is a view that can only be beneficial to librarians and information officers. In fact, the notion of the value chain, arose from the strategic question of how to best employ IT (Information Technology) to enhance competitiveness and was devised as an analytical tool to use in determining where best to examine the potential application of IT.

Second, the notion of the value chain is a powerful diagnostic tool for librarians. A very useful exercise is for one key person on the library team to analyze the relative importance of the value chain's components to the organization as a whole while another key person to analyzes the proportion of library service supporting each component. Then, the library management team can examine the two estimates and evaluate whether the library's services are being directed to those areas that are most critical to the organization's users, and if not, why not? Are the library's resources and services being diverted to non-critical areas? Are opportunities that may support the organization in key areas being missed? Note the similarity here to the concept of critical success factors, discussed under Enterprise Wide Information Analysis.

Key Article:

Brown, Eryn. "The Push to Streamline Supply Chains." *Fortune* 135, no. 4 (March 1997): 108-111.

* *

ENTERPRISE RESOURCE PLANNING (ERP)

Enterprise Resource Planning is the name for use of one very large (and very expensive) but modularized commercial data management package to integrate an organization's handling of its internal data. The name is confusing, a much better one would be Enterprise Information Integration Systems, or simply Enterprise Systems, and the latter term is beginning to be used more often. At the moment though, ERP is still the buzzword. The emergence of ERP has been concurrent with the emergence of SAP and its system R12 for mainframe computers and R13 for the now more typical client server environment, the German company that largely developed the concept, now with other contenders from Oracle, Baan, and People-Soft.

The idea behind ERP is to replace all of an organization's old legacy systems that communicated poorly with each other and that stored information in different formats, with one flexible but totally integrated system. That allowed one to share information and to analyze it in almost any conceivable fashion. One could say that data warehousing is one approach to numerous legacy systems and incompatible data – take the data from various legacy systems, reformat it, and put it into a large all encompassing data warehouse. While, the ERP approach is to scrap the legacy systems and adapt one new large enterprise system for the organization, an integrated system designed from the beginning for data sharing and analysis. In addition, an ERP is designed to support and perform all of the transactions a company needs to undertake, not just to share data and to store it.

The wisdom of using ERPs in much debated. The attraction is one integrated system designed to do everything with all data treated homogeneously. The cons are the expense of implementation and possible regulations in the systems, which after all is not designed for your organization, but designed to be generic, though with extensive options to tailor it to your organization. What if your organization does something a little differently and that is your competitive advantage? Do you write your own endorsements and risk unintended consequences in a system that you have not developed and where therefore it may be difficult to anticipate consequences? Do you ask the vendor for a features enhancement that your competition may learn to use? In any case, such enhancements in a system so complex are also apt to be very difficult for the vendor to implement.

ERP and the Librarian

At its most obvious level, ERP concerns internal information, and the librarian is the expert in external information, and the overlap is minor, although clearly, the implementation of any IT system that effects the organization so profoundly, and occasionally as traumatically as ERP does, is something that the librarian should be cognizant of. There is more to it than that for the librarian however. ERP should not be implemented without a serious study as to the pros and cons, and top management should be heavily involved in that study. The librarian can make a strong case for involvement in that study. A major thread in the development of more sophisticated information handling in the corporation is the increased integration and joint use of internal and external information. The librarian, the expert on external information can therefore make a strong case for inclusion on that study team.

Key Article:

Davenport, Thomas H. "Putting the Enterprise into the Enterprise System". *Harvard Business Review* 76, no. 4 (July–August 1998): 121-131.

* *

INFORMATION DRIVEN MARKETING
("Relationship Marketing")

Relationship Marketing is simply using information to target potential customers more precisely, tailoring services to specific customers more effectively, and individualizing communications with customers. The phrases "targeted marketing" or "individualized marketing" are probably more descriptive, but relationship marketing is the phrase that has gained popularity in the business community. The presumption is that the use of such individualized communications and services engenders a long-term relationship with the customer. The relationship breeds customer loyalty, repeat business, and creates a barrier to competition. The salient point to us is that the central core of these themes is information driven.

The emergence of the phrase also reflects the growing realization that by combining an organization's data about its customers with data available externally about those customers, an organization can tailor its marketing much more effectively. An example which illustrates the concept concerns Bloomingdale's, a department store in the United States which caters to relatively affluent customers, and which has gained a reputation for being a style leader. Bloomingdale's ("Bloomies") also does substantial business through a number of mail order catalogs. Bloomingdale's realized that customers who had recently relocated might be shopping for new furniture - perhaps they had bought a larger home, or perhaps they had relocated from California to New England and their old furniture was architecturally incompatible with their new house. Bloomingdale's used external data sources, such as post office change of address files and motor vehicle registration files alongside customer supplied information to identify and locate customers who had recently moved. Bloomingdale's promptly sent the potential customers an individualized letter and a catalog specifically featuring furniture. The result was a substantial increase in furniture sales. The example illustrates the salient points of relationship marketing.

- The combination of internal and external data.
- A service or promotion targeted to specific customers who match specific criteria. Ideally, the service or promotion provides a real added value to those customers.
- The establishment, maintenance, or reinforcement of a longer term "relationship" with the customer.

This area seems to be a particularly fertile field for acronyms and buzzwords. One is CRM, Customer Relationship Management. Another is ECR, Efficient Consumer Response. The former is simply shorthand for relationship marketing. The later is the closely related concept of using information about customers to reach them efficiently. In particular, that means, as in the Bloomingdale's example, targeting particular customers with marketing approaches that are particularly suited to their particular circumstances and preferences, rather than wholesale, one size fits all, indiscriminate mass mailing.

Relationship Marketing and the Librarian

The librarian's potential role in relationship marketing is significant. The librarian is, or should be, the organization's internal expert on external data and external data files. The organization's MIS (Management Information Systems) staff on whom the marketing department has traditionally relied for IT (Information Technology) support, typically knows the T (technology) but not the I (information), and what information they do know is almost entirely internal not external. Market researchers often know some external information sources, but they often know them very specifically and very narrowly, and they are not trained, as librarians are, in locating others. The Bloomingdale's example above illustrates an important point about relationship marketing. It often involves non-traditional, according to the organization, external information sources. Therein lies the librarian's opportunity, ideally not only to locate, but also to suggest those information sources.

To respond proactively and not just reactively, the librarian must become involved with the marketing effort. This requires the librarian to communicate and liaise with the marketing staff, and in the best situation, the librarian participates as an integral part of those marketing brainstorming and planning sessions. A memo, or a lunch convention with an opinion leader in marketing about the contributions you can make would be the best opening to turn this recent publicity and enthusiasm for relationship marketing to the librarian's advantage.

Key Article:

Bessen, John. "Riding the Marketing Information Wave." *Harvard Business Review* 71, no. 5 (September/October 1993): 150-160.

* * *

KNOWLEDGE MANAGEMENT AND INTELLECTUAL CAPITAL

Knowledge Management is the hottest topic to hit librarianship since online searching. There are various definitions of it - one good one is "the broad process of locating, organizing, and transferring, and using the information and expertise within an organization"[1], another is "the process of capturing a company's collective expertise".[2]

In one sense, we can argue that Knowledge Management is simply librarianship applied to the operations of an organization, whether a for-profit consulting firm, such as Andersen or a non-profit organization such as the World Bank. Knowledge Management evolved from the combination of two factors: the early and mid 1990s enthusiasm for "intellectual capital" and the appearance of corporate Intranets. "Intellectual Capital is the growing awareness that information is a factor of production, in a category with land, labor, capital, and energy".[3] In the early and mid 1990s there was an increasing awareness in the business community that knowledge was an important organizational resource that needed to be nurtured, sustained, and if possible accounted for. Peter Drucker, as he commonly does, put it perhaps most compellingly

> We now know that the source of wealth is something, specifically human knowledge. If we apply knowledge to tasks that we obviously know how to do, we call it productivity. If we apply knowledge to tasks that are new and different, we call it innovation. Only knowledge allows us to achieve those two goals.[4]

Information continues to be an extraordinarily diffuse and nebulous thing to try to quantify, measuring and accounting for it (in the sense of the accounting profession) continues to be a daunting task. Despite relatively modest progress in that quarter, the Intellectual Capital movement was successful in bringing the importance of information as "a factor of production", as economists would phrase it, to the attention of management.

The Internet's explosion during the 1990s corresponded with the Intellectual Capital movement. The business world realized that Internet technology and procedures could be used to link an organization together. Using the Internet and its conventions for data display and access, and limiting access to the members of an organization, results in an "Intranet". Companies had used LANS, Local Area Networks, and WANS, Wide Area Networks, for some time but, Internet based Intranets were far easier to set up and administer, and the tools for employees to put information on the net and to access it were far superior.

The first organizations to fully realize the potential of Intranets were typically the large, worldwide consulting firms who had long realized that the commodity they dealt in was information and knowledge. These firms saw the Intranet as an ideal tool with which to share and disseminate knowledge throughout their organizations' scattered offices. The phrase they chose to describe the Intranet based systems they were developing was "knowledge management". How can a consultant in Valparaiso, Chile, working for an company headquartered in Chicago be made aware of work done by another consultant in Stockholm,

---

[1] http://www.apqc.org/b2/b2.htm

[2] Justin Hibbard, "Knowing What We Know", *Information_Week* (October 20, 1997): 46-64.

[3] Eduardo Talero and Philip Gaudette, *Harnessing Information for Development: World Bank Group Vision and Strategy*, Draft Document, (Washington, D.C.: The World Bank, July 1995).

[4] Hibbard, 46.

work that the Valparaiso consultant could use to respond authoritatively and convincingly to a request for a proposal and be awarded the contract? The best current answer to that problem is a worldwide intranet based knowledge sharing system, i.e. Knowledge Management.

The Knowledge Management notion is also closely linked to the concept of the "Learning Organization". In fact, they can be described as different facets of the same thesis. The Learning Organization is the argument that what ultimately creates and distinguishes a successful organization is the success in creating and sharing information and knowledge, in short its success at learning. The obvious corollary is that to be successful, an organization must create a culture that fosters learning. One can say, to summarize perhaps too glibly, that the concept of the Learning Organization focuses on the creation of knowledge, while Knowledge Management focuses on the acquisition, structuring, retention, and dissemination of that knowledge. The overlap is the area of sharing knowledge and in stressing the need for creating an organizational climate, which encourages and rewards that sharing. The seminal piece of literature is the book by Peter Senge, *The Fifth Discipline, the Art and Practice of the Learning Organization.*

A new term that has recently emerged is FLO, the Faster Learning Organization. This is the goal of knowledge management, to create a FLO that will thereby have a major competitive advantage over other organizations. In the words of Skip Le Faure, Senior Vice President of General Motors Corporation, and President of General Motors University, and previously chairman of GM's Saturn division: "The only long term competitive advantage that a company has is how effectively it manages its competitive knowledge".[5]

Another important perception that has accelerated the enthusiasm for Knowledge Management has been the richness and reach thesis of Evans and Wurster. They pointed out in the Sept./Oct. 1997 issue of Harvard Business Review that the nature of communications had dramatically changed. Their observation is that until now, one had a choice of richness or reach in communication, but one could not achieve both simultaneously. A face-to-face conversation for example was rich in content, nuance, and interactivity, but its reach was small, one or at most a few persons. A mass mailing or radio of TV broadcast had great reach, but was thin on content, nuance, and interactivity. Communication strategies were always an either/or choice.

Now with the Internet, they argue, we can craft systems that simultaneously provide both richness and reach, and this transforms not only how we think about communications, but also how we think about organizations and how they do business. This thesis, which is in a sense an instantiation of Gibson and Jackson's Domain III, Transformation, and Koenig's Stage III, has been incorporated into the canon of Knowledge Management as a very persuasive argument as to why the time is right for a thorough rethink of how information and knowledge is shared in the organization.[6] Further it can be argued that the removal of the richness or reach dichotomy means that changes will not be gradual and incremental, but that they will be major and dramatic. The organization that does not keep up risks being left very far behind, and possibly being out of business very quickly.
In fact, Knowledge Management has expanded to become a portmanteau term intended to include all of the positive aspects of the management fads of the last decade and a half, while

[5] Presentation to the Conference Board Conference, "The 1998 Conference on Knowledge Management and Organizational Learning", Chicago, Illinois, 15 April 1998.

[6] See section titled "Information Systems Stage Hypotheses".

avoiding the excesses. The Knowledge Management Framework (figure 2) is a very useful graphic visualization. This graphic, promoted by IBM, conveys particularly well how broad the concept of knowledge management has become in the business community.

Figure 2. Knowledge Management Framework

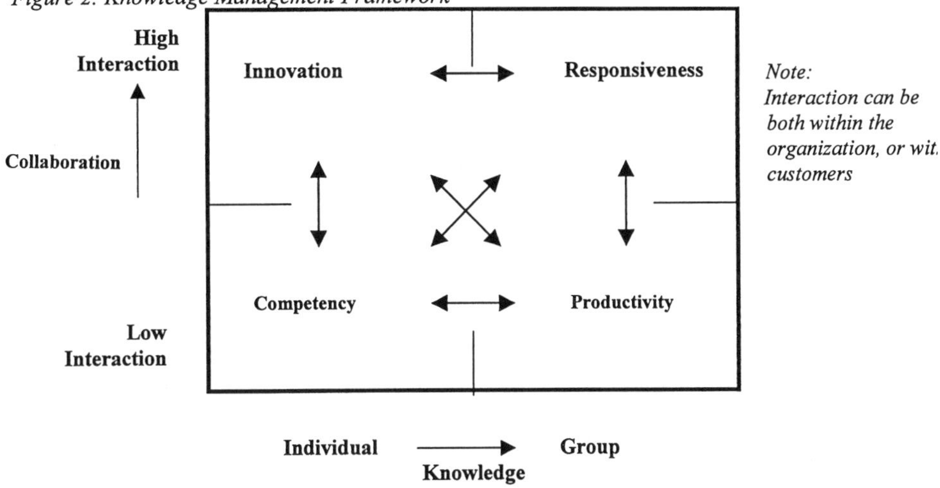

What this is intended to represent is – as Knowledge Management enhances knowledge sharing and collaboration, the results achieved are:

- Innovation, in areas of high interaction and individual knowledge
- Competency, in areas of low interaction and individual knowledge
- Responsiveness, in areas of high interaction and group knowledge
- Productivity, in areas of low interaction and group knowledge.

Figure 3. The Knowledge Management Progression

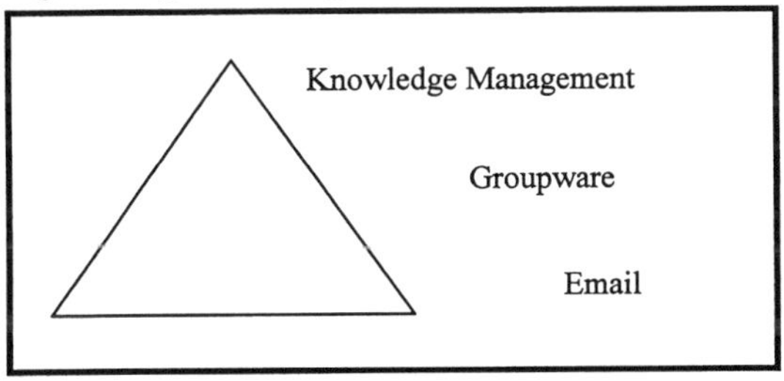

The Knowledge Management Progression (figure 3) is another useful graphic aid to thinking about knowledge management. The idea here is that typically the first extensive use of information technology to enhance knowledge sharing is the widespread use of email. Then comes broad use of groupware, software designed to help teams work together in an electronic environment. The epitome is true knowledge management, including a transformation in the culture of the organization to encourage and reward information creation and sharing.

The Librarian and Knowledge Management

It is important first to recognize that "knowledge management" has rapidly become a broad and generic term. Its meaning in the business community now is much more than the capture, organization, retrieval and delivery of information and knowledge that we would naturally interpret the term to mean. Indeed it has become much broader than what the consulting firms had in mind when they coined the term. In fact there is beginning to be a reaction in business circles that the term knowledge management is not the ideal phrase. Some persons maintain that it is both too specific for a concept that is really much broader, and also that it is perhaps somewhat impolitic. Users, employees, and customers do not particularly relish the notion that their knowledge is being managed, rather they would prefer terminology that would imply that the are being supported in their undertakings. One of many phrases that has been suggested to replace knowledge management is "knowledge sharing", another is "knowledge networking". One can see a parallel here of the terminological shift from MIS, Management Information System to DSS, Decision Support Systems. On the other hand, IBM's use of and support for the term knowledge management may standardize the term just as it did for the term "word processing".

What are the major themes running through what the business community understands knowledge management to be?

- ***Silos***

This is the hot new buzzword. How do you integrate the silos? Silo is used here as a metaphor for the too self-contained unit into which stuff gets dumped and taken out but does no communication with the other silos (products, regions, divisions, units, etc.) that constitute the organization. The solution to silos is to create communities and thereby further collaboration.

- ***Communities and Collaboration***

Most of the concrete applications of knowledge management described to date consist of creating and supporting communities of shared interest and information need. These communities might be sales representatives in a pharmaceutical company or those persons at the World Bank and among their customers interested in ground transport and logistics. In some cases, as in the former, the community exists formally and hierarchically or, as in the latter, it exists informally and horizontally. At the World Bank for example there are now approximately seventy "knowledge areas" grouped into fifteen larger sections; at IBM there are forty-nine "competency networks". The intended consequence of knowledge management support for the communities is not only knowledge sharing, but also collaboration, and thereby of course productivity.

- ***Tacit Knowledge***

Tacit knowledge is now the term used for the knowledge that is in people's heads or in their own files, as distinguished from explicit knowledge that exits in documents or databases. Current knowledge management thinking is almost entirely about establishing the structure and the climate to enable and encourage those who have knowledge to share it. There is close to no mention of capturing tacit knowledge in the now somewhat tarnished sense of artificial intelligence and the "knowledge engineer" who would capture the expertise of the expert on diesel/electric locomotive repair trouble shooting before he retired. What there typically is, is the encouragement and the establishment of systems to enable the employee to submit a "best practice" description of how they accomplish something so that others can use that knowledge. The information may be reviewed and edited before it goes on the system (particularly so for pharmaceutical companies who are subject to governmental approval concerning what they may say about a therapeutic agent), but it is input by the user, not be a knowledge manger or knowledge engineer.

This is an important point for librarians to recognize, that there has been substantial disillusionment in the business community with the very much over-hyped "artificial intelligence" and with the software packages and consulting firms that promised to set up AI systems for companies. There have been AI successes to be sure, but they have been at the tactical and near clerical level, monitoring credit card transactions for plausibility or likely misuse for example. The successes have not been at the strategic level envisioned by the proponents of knowledge management nor have they been of the collaborative synergistic kind yielding competitive advantage. Librarians can make a contribution here, but we must be careful to phrase our proposed contributions in terms of making tacit knowledge accessible. Be very careful about suggesting that you are going to capture it and streamline it. Yes, an index or a thesaurus is a syndetic structure, but such phraseology will resonate poorly and make you sound like a naive proponent of AI, someone who if listened to will cost money and yield little in the way of results.

- ***Incentives and Rewards***

Effective knowledge sharing requires rewarding those who input information into the system and contribute something useful. Otherwise, what motivation do employees have to contribute information that will, for example, improve the performance of other sales representatives relative to their own? Changing compensation and incentive systems is not something that organizations do readily; it is an undertaking fraught with peril and with unintended and often unfortunate consequences. A frequent complaint among knowledge management officers is how slow and difficult it is to get top management to make such changes.

This does not impact librarians directly, after all, information sharing is what we were hired for. But, as the importance of information creation and sharing is better recognized in the organization, then we can hope for some spillover effort to those who facilitate and make possible that information creation and sharing. For that positive spillover to take effect however, we must have achieved recognition as key players in the knowledge management process.

- ***Customer Knowledge***

A pervasive theme in business discussion of Knowledge Management is the importance of including the customer in the scope of knowledge management systems so as to include and leverage this expertise. This is considered key for a number of reasons:

- better and more timely design of new products and services
- early warning and competitive intelligence
- customers commitment and loyalty
- the synergy of collaboration.

The emphasis here is upon the exchange of knowledge, ideas, and opinions, for example, not just the data currently exchanged with just-in-time inventory or supply chain management.

- ***Top Management Support and Change Agentry***

Another major theme is that Knowledge Management is about a whole new way of operating, a transformation of the organization.[7] As such knowledge management requires knowledge management professionals to be change agents, and that in turn requires top management support, and better yet is the direct involvement of top management if the effort is to be successful.

The obvious corollary here is that knowledge management is going to be an exciting place to be, not somewhere or something, which we can afford to be left out of.

Finally, there is:

- ***Trust, Human Relations, and a recognition of Social Capital***

This is perhaps a trifle surprising. At one level this may be an attempt to tie knowledge management to the justified recoil from the excesses of downsizing and rightsizing frequently justified under the guise of business process reengineering, but it is also quite logical. Good communication and extensive knowledge sharing are not likely to happen unless there is an atmosphere of trust and some commitment to the employee. Knowledge Management is in effect being presented as the antidote to the trust lost and the knowledge lost in ill conceived and ill executed rightsizings when valuable employees were let go, their knowledge going with them, and with a reservoir of mistrust and insecurity left behind. As Larry Prusak bluntly puts it "re-engineering is the enemy of knowledge".[8]

Social Capital is another facet of the same recognition. In this business context, social capital is operationally defined as those behavioral norms that lower transaction costs and enable cooperation. What norm better to enhance communications, transactions, and cooperation than trust. It is interesting to observe that at the same time there is an increasing recognition at the macro economic level of the importance of trust and consistency in enabling and expediting international trade and for encouraging foreign direct investment.

In another sense, social capital is what has been added to intellectual capital to create knowledge management. Intellectual capital was originally defined as having two major components, the information itself, information capital, and structured capital, the mechanisms to take advantage of the information capital, the mechanisms to capture, store, retrieve, communicate information etc. It was easy to see our role in the structured capital. Later, when it was realized that the organizations intranet could be constructed so as to include customers and that this had major benefits (see above), customers capital was frequently added as a component of intellectual capital and presented the following diagram.

---

[7] See the Gibson and Jackson stage hypothesis in the section on Stage Hypothesis Information Systems.

[8] Larry Prusak, Managing Principal, IBM Global Services, Consulting Group Presentation to the Conference Board Conference, "The 1998 Conference on Knowledge Management and Organizational Learning", Chicago, Illinois, 16, April, 1998.

Figure 4. Intellectual Capital

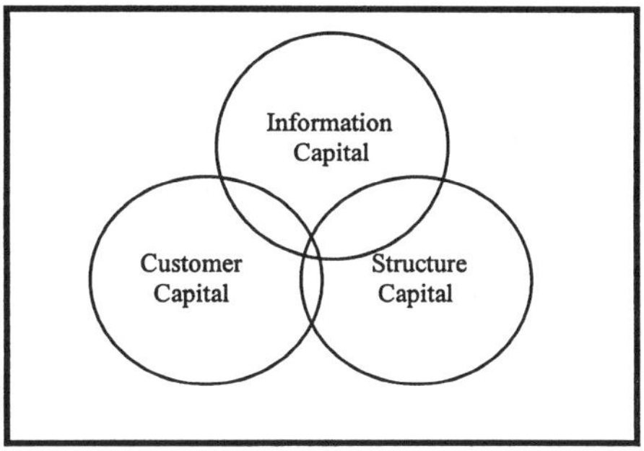

This however was always an awkward sort of diagram, mixing apples with oranges. Now the trendy diagram is that Knowledge Management has three components, thus, according to Prusak of IBM.

Figure 5. Knowledge Capital Components

Knowledge Resources	+	**Social Capital**	+	**Infrastructure**
• Explicit • Tacit • Formal • Informal		• Culture • Trust • Knowledge Behavior • Human Capital Issues		• Processes • Resources • Technology • Metrics

Lest the discussions of all the issues that have crept into knowledge management be too off-putting, the graphic above is reassuring. Librarians certainly have major contributions to make in both knowledge resources and in infrastructure. In social capital, the library is often perceived as a neutral and non-threatening institution in which one can have trust.

One obvious question is – is this enthusiasm for knowledge management a flash in the pan, or is it here to stay? For those of us in the library and information profession perhaps the most compelling bellweather indicators of the business community's perception of the importance of knowledge management are these:

- in its 1997 annual report, Lon Gerstner said that his goal was "to turn IBM into the world's premier Knowledge Management Company", and
- the president of Donaldson, Lufkin, Jenrette stated recently that not only do Knowledge Management systems add value to a company, but that DLJ analysts specifically look for the existence of KM when analyzing a company's worth and its stock value.

These are anecdotal points to be sure, but they are certainly strong indications that knowledge management is here in a big way, and that it is likely to stay here.

Rules to Remember in Seeking a Larger Role in Knowledge Management

- You can make a contribution in regard to tacit knowledge (a hot topic), but describe your potential role as enhancing access to it. Be very careful about suggesting that you will capture it and organize it. Do not get tarred with the brush of artificial intelligence.
- Emphasize knowledge sharing and collaboration.
- Use the Knowledge Capital Components metaphor:

Knowledge Resources	+	**Social Capital**	+	**Infrastructure**

- Knowledge Management will be an exciting process. It is not something we want to be left out of. For a librarian to be left out of knowledge management may well result in being left out of the organization.

Key articles relating to ***Intellectual Capital*** and Background for ***Knowledge Management***:

The business literature:

Botkin, J. and Davis, S. "The Coming of Knowledge-based Business." *Harvard Business Review*, 72, no. 5 (1994): 165-207.

Brooking, Annie. "The Management of Intellectual Capital." *Long Range Planning* 30 (June 1997): 364-365.

Darling, M.S. "Building the Knowledge Organization." *Business Quarterly*, 61, no.2 (1996): 61-66.

Drucker, P.F. "The Age of Social Transformation." *The Atlantic Monthly*, 274, no.11 (November 1994): 53-80.
Not about Intellectual Capital per se, but a marvelously insightful essay on the importance of information in the future.

Edvinsson, Leif. "Developing Intellectual Capital at Skandia." *Long Range Planning* 30 (June 1997): 366-373.

Edvinsson, Leif, and Michael S. Malone. *Intellectual Capital: Realizing Your Company's True Value by Finding Its Hidden Roots*. New York: Harper Business, 1997.

Evans, Phillip B., and Thomas S. Wurster. "Strategy and the New Economics of Information." *Harvard Business Review* 75, no. 5 (1987): 70-82.
The "richness and reach" hypothesis.

Kaplan, R.S. and Norton, D.P. "The Balanced Scorecard – Measures that Drive Performance." *Harvard Business Review* 70, no. 1 (1992): 71-79.

Not about Intellectual Capital per se, but an influential article that stresses the inadequacies of traditional financial measures of performance, and discusses some possible measures of innovation and learning.

Nonaka, Ikujiro, and Hirotaka, Takeuchi. *The Knowledge Creating Company.* New York & Oxford: Oxford University Press, 1995.

Reich, R. "The Real Economy." *The Atlantic Monthly*, 267, no. 2 (1991): 35-52.

Senge, Peter M. *The Fifth Discipline: The Art and Practice of the Learning Organization.* New York: Doubleday/Currency, 1990.

Stewart, Thomas A. *Intellectual Capital: The New Wealth of Organizations.* New York: Doubleday/Currency, 1997.

Stewart, Thomas A. "Brainpower." *Fortune* 123 (June 3, 1991): 44-60.

Stewart, Thomas A. "Now Capital Means Brains, not just Bucks." *Fortune* 123 (January 1991): 31-32.

Stewart, Thomas A. "Your Company's Most Valuable Asset: Intellectual Capital." *Fortune* 130 (October 3, 1994): 68-74.

Stewart, Thomas A. "Getting Real about Brainpower." *Fortune* 132 (November 27, 1995): 201-203.

Stewart is clearly the key proponent of the intellectual capital concept in the business world. Reading two or three of his most recent articles is sufficient; they include all the concepts of the earlier pieces.

***The library literature*:**

Key pieces in the library literature that relates to intellectual capital (in many cases predating the business world's discovery of intellectual capital) that one may be able to use both for leverage and to document the role and the legitimacy of librarianship in the domain of intellectual capital.

Burk, C.F. Jr., and Horton, F.W. Jr. *InfoMap: A Complete Guide to Discovering Your Information Resources*, Prentice-Hall, Englewood Cliffs, NJ, 1988.

Horton, F.W. Jr. "Mapping Corporate Information Resources," *International Journal of Information Management*, first of three articles: 8, no. 4 (1988): 249-259.

Horton, F.W. Jr. "Mapping Corporate Information Resources," *International Journal of Information Management*, second of three articles: 9, no. 1 (1988): 19-24.

Horton, F.W. Jr. "Mapping Corporate Information Resources," *International Journal of Information Management*, third of three articles: 9, no. 2 (1989): 91-95.

Orna, E. *Practical Information Policies: How to Manage Information Flow in*

Organizations, Gower, Aldershot, 1990.
Orna is still the best and most practical guide to information auditing.
Read Horton and Orna; it will give ideas about and tools for info-mapping (Horton) and information auditing (Orna) that the business folks have not thought about yet.

Special Libraries Association, *The Information Audit*, Special Libraries Association, Washington, DC, 1996.
A collection of essays by various authors about the information audit. Not, unfortunately as good as it might be; neither Orna nor Horton are contributors.

Badenoch, D. *et al*. "The Value of Information," in Feeney, M. and Grieves, M. eds., *The Value and Impact of Information*, New York: Bowker-Saur, 1994.

Koenig, M.E.D. "The Importance of Information Services for Productivity – under recognized, and under investigate." *Special Libraries* 83, no. 4 (1992): 199-210.

Koenig, M.E.D. "Intellectual Capital and Knowledge Management." *IFLA Journal* 22, no. 4 (1996): 299-301.

Koenig, M.E.D. "Intellectual Capital and How to Leverage IT." *The Bottom Line* 10, no. 3 (1997): 112-118.

Edvinsson, Leif. "Visualizing Intellectual Capital in Skandia." (Supplement) *Skandia's 1994 Annual Report*. Stockholm, Sweden: Skandia AFS, 1995.
The most frequently mentioned and exhibited example of trying to qualify and report on intellectual capital.

Knowledge Management:
(Note: there is more material written in the last two years than any one person can digest.)

Broadbent, Marianne. "The Phenomenon of Knowledge Management: What Does it meant to the Library Profession." *Information Outlook* 2, no. 5 (May 1998): 23-36.
Brooking, Annie. *Intellectual Capital*. London, New York: International Thomson Business Press, 1997.

Davenport, Thomas H., and Laurence Prusak. *Information Econology: Mastering the Information and Knowledge Environment*. New York: Oxford University Press, 1997.

Davenport, Thomas H., and Laurence Prusak. *Working Knowledge: How Organizations Manage What They Know*. Boston, Mass.: Harvard Business School Press, 1998.
Prusak is one of the few business writers who is reasonably knowledgeable about and sympathetic to libraries.

Myers, Paul S., ed. *Knowledge Management and Organizational Design*. Resources for the Knowledge Based Economy. Boston, Mass.: Butterworth Heinemann, 996.

Web sites:

American Productivity and Quality Center
(http://www.apqc.org/)

@Brint: Knowledge Management and Organizational Learning
(http://www.brint.com/OrgLrng.htm)

CIO Magazine Online
(http://www.cio.com/archive/)

Graduate School of Business, University of Texas at Austin
(http://www.bus.utexas.edu/kman/answers/htm)

Institute for Intellectual Capital
(http://scholars.ivey.uwo.ca/nbontis/ic)

Knowledge Inc.
(http://www.knowledgeinc.com/quantera)

Knowledge Magazine
(http://www.media-access.com/publications.html)

Knowledge Praxis
(http://www.media-access.com/whatis.html#history)

Organizational Knowledge Media
(http://kmi.open.ac.uk/~simonb/org-knowledge/)

Stanford Learning Organization Web
(http://www-leland.stanford.edu/group/SLOW/)

* * *

DATA WAREHOUSING / DATA MINING

The concept of Data Warehousing and Data Mining is both basic and broad, and the two phrases are used to mean various things in various contexts. Data Warehousing may at first appear to be the passive stockpiling of data, but rather it is the assembling of selected, filtered, and structured data from a variety of sources into one coherent assembly for the purpose of being able to find meaningful relationships within that data. Data Mining is the attempt to extract useful relationships from within large bodies of data.

The notion behind the enthusiasm is that if an organization can assemble and combine the data on its operations that it collects, most likely with external information as well, then an organization can discover meaningful and useful patterns in that data. To make up an example, assume that an automobile manufacturer has data on its sales and customers, and combines that data with automobile registration data from the motor vehicle authority along with purchase information from a major chain of discount department stores and grocery stores. That automobile manufacturer might be able to find some very useful predictive correlation between the purchase patterns of consumers for general merchandise, clothing, or sporting equipment, and the purchase of certain types of automobiles, for example the sports utility vehicle. Perhaps it is the case that individuals that have not bought a new car in the last five years, who purchase more than the average amount of sports equipment and an unusually high proportion of frozen and pre-prepared foods are unusually likely to buy a new sports utility vehicle. That would be very useful marketing information for an automobile manufacturer who was introducing a sports utility vehicle. It would enable a very targeted marketing campaign. Note the relationship between data warehousing and data mining with information driven marketing (relationship marketing). The principle motivation behind data warehousing and the data mining is to unearth information that will produce a competitive advantage in marketing.

Though the basic concept behind data warehousing and data mining is simple enough, the implementation is not so easy and is not inexpensive. One cannot simply throw huge masses of data together and make a rich stew of it. Typically a data warehousing project is based on relational database technology and the relational concept of data structuring. In practice this typically means selecting various data files (both internal to the organization and acquired from outside), selecting the salient data fields from within the various file structures, stripping and cleaning the data (frequently a far more complex task than is typically assumed beforehand), linking the data, and designing a relational database structure to map the data onto. Once the data has been combined in a meaningful fashion, then relationships can be looked for, and “what if” or “is it the case that” questions can be asked.

Once the data from various files has been combined (it may be combined in a relatively rigorous fashion, as described above, or it may be loosely linked by a program that looks for common identifiers, such as driver’s license numbers or tax registration numbers). There are programs that will tirelessly massage the data and look for relationships that might be useful. Perhaps, again making up an example, such a program might find that there was a strong correlation between the propensity to buy sport utility vehicles and 1) a relatively recent diminution in the purchase of baby foods, and 2) the purchase of pesto sauce. No one would probably have thought to look for such a relationship, but a search program can evaluate tens of thousands of such combinations and report on the ones that appear to have some relational significance.

The social ramifications of data warehousing and data mining are non-trivial. There are now companies that specialize in acquiring huge amounts of data from disparate sources, finding relationships and selling their results. The problem is of course that what links the disparate data is the identification of the particular customers, you or me. What constraints society should put on such assemblages of data is a question that needs analysis and resolution.

Data Warehousing / Data Mining and the Librarian

The librarian is (or should be) the expert on external data and where and how to obtain it. Their most obvious potential role is in suggesting and helping in the acquisition of such data. A second possible role is in designing the structure of the data warehouse. However, this consists of structuring data not in the bibliographic sense, but in the relational sense of databases, third and fourth normal data forms, etc. If the librarian is not familiar with these concepts, they should become familiar with them before venturing too far into the area of data warehousing and data mining.

Key Articles:

Data Warehousing / Data Mining:
Darling, Charles B. "Dataming for the Masses." *Datamation* 43, no. 2 (February 1997): 52-55.

Relational Data Structuring Concepts:
Koenig, M.E.D. "Data Relationships: Information Retrieval Systems and Database Management Systems." *Information Technology and Libraries* 4, no. 3 (September 1985): 247-272.

A word of warning is that we librarians have begun to use these phrases in a fashion that is specific to our realm and that would not be recognized by most persons in the business community. Librarians have started using the phrase to mean what is basically an extension of multi-database searching and retrieved item matching. This searching is typically not of the organization's data, but of traditional online databases and of the Internet. This is not how the term is understood outside the library community, and if we are not careful about how and with whom we use these phrases. We can easily appear very naïve and out of touch.

Examples of librarians use of these phrases:

Tragert, Joseph. "Enhancing Information Retrieval: New Data Mining Techniques Internally and Across the Internet." Presentation at the National Online Meeting, New York, N.Y., 14 May 1998.

Anderson, Steven B., and Robert S. Lundquist. "Application of Database Warehouse Technologies for Quality Control within the Information Industry." In *Proceedings of the 19th National Online Meeting*, 27-36. Martha Williams, ed., Medford NJ, U.S.A.: Information Today, 1998.

* *

CORE COMPETENCIES

The notion of core competencies is the argument that each organization has its own core competencies, areas in which the organization's performance excels. The organization should insofar as practical, focus on its core competencies, and consider outsourcing, purchasing from outside, those goods or activities which are necessary to the organization's activities, but are not within its area of core competencies.

The basic idea is not new. An automobile manufacturer, whose core competencies may include automobile engines and chaises, may be better advised to buy window and windshield glass from a company that specializes in making glass, i.e. whose core competency is making glass, rather than the automobile manufacturer making the glass in its own factories. What is new is the recognition that information technology and communication technology is rapidly changing the balance between making it in-house, rather than buying it from an outside supplier.

The key reference for this concept is the *Harvard Business Review* article by Prahalad & Hamel, which appeared in 1990. It quickly became recognized as a seminal piece, and the phrase "core competencies" became a basic piece of one's business vocabulary. A clear example that Prahalad and Hamel use is that Honda's core competence is the design and building of engine and drive trains, whether that is meant to be used in an automobile or an electric generator, a motorcycle, or a lawn mower. Honda's core competence is <u>not</u> the automobile. The notion of core competence is contrasted with the "old model" of the SBU, the strategic business unit, based on market and product. The core competence notion implies that the company develops the products and enters the markets for which its core competencies provide opportunity. Whereas, the previous notion of the SBU tended to start with the market segment as the target, and from that to determine what products, what competencies, what logistics, etc were needed.

The core competency notion is intimately related to the "hierarchies to markets" theme.[9] Just as advances in information technology move the balance from central planning and hierarchies, at the same time they make it easier to outsource. Therefore information technology makes it easier and more attractive to contract out those things which are not core competencies, and makes it more imperative that the company concentrate on and remain competitive in its core competencies.

Core Competencies and the Librarian

At its most basic level this is a hot topic, a hot phrase that the librarian must be able to use correctly in order to sound current. Furthermore though, it is relevant to the librarian in two very specific ways. First, the librarian must be familiar with what his firm's core competencies are and what senior management views them to be (that may not always be the same). The best way to ensure support for the library functions and its survival is to link the libraries services with the organization's core competencies and to make sure that the link is visible and appreciated.

Second, in this era of rapid change, it is useful for the librarian to ask the following questions:

- What are my core competencies and what are the core competencies of my unit?

---

[9]See the discussion on "Hierarchies to Markets".

- Am I concentrating my effort or my department's effort on core competencies?
- Am I spending too much time on things like filing or other services and functions that can be outsourced?
- Indeed, as I look at my operations, are there things that I should suggest be outsourced?

It may be much better for the librarian to suggest outsourcing some functions and receive credit for being a good manager, rather than have someone else offer the identical solution and possibly conclude that the entire library operation is an opportunity for outsourcing.

Key Article:

Prahalad, C.K., and Hamel, Gary. "The Core Competence of the Corporation." *Harvard Business Review* 68, no. 3 (May-June, 1990): 79-91.

* * *

BUSINESS PROCESS RE-ENGINEERING

Business Process Reengineering was the hot topic in the business community in the mid 1990s. It simply meant redesigning the operations and the workflow of organization to take advantage of the capabilities of electronic communications. Those capabilities such as real time operation and the distance independence of modern electronic information systems permitted radical redesign and in many cases dramatic rationalization and simplification of business procedures and systems.

Though electronic business systems have grown incrementally in capability for many years, why did the enthusiasm for business process reengineering burst upon the scene so suddenly? There are three reasons. First, most business systems had been relatively local at the department level. The linking together of systems and the access to systems elsewhere in the organization because of the operational emergence of networking, local area networks (LANs), the Internet, and corporate intranets, revealed new possibilities and opened peoples eyes to those prospects. Second, the limitations of print-on-paper technology (the central file for example, accessible in only one geographic location) had been with us for decades and consequently we took for granted the organizational designs and procedures those limitations forced upon us. At some point those psychological blinders had to fall, and the arrival of widely and economically available networking capability was the catalyst that caused them to fall.[10] Finally the climate of business, the increasing internationalization and specialization of business, trends which were to a large extent themselves driven by the increasing capabilities of information technology[11] were forcing business organizations to become leaner and more competitive, and business process reengineering was a powerful tool to accomplish that.

Business Process Reengineering acquired something of a bad name, because it frequently has been associated with the downsizing of organization and the consequent laying-off of employees, which needless to say are very unpopular. Another criticism was that in many cases in their enthusiasm to "rightsize", a euphemism for downsize, and make themselves more profitable by reducing costs, organizations often divested themselves of key mid level employees who took their expertise and knowledge, their “intellectual capital” with them.

The salient fact remains however that improved information technology and access to information can allow an organization to dramatically change its way of doing business, its processes and procedures, and the entire structure of the organization. There is indeed a fascinating parallel between business process reengineering and data driven design systems.[12] Data driven systems design was the realization that the structure of a complex data processing system was driven by the flow of information within that system. Business process reengineering is the realization that the very structure of a business organization likewise can be and should be driven by the flow of information within the organization. The limitations of print-on-paper technology have prevented us from realizing that goal, but now network technology is removing those limitations, and opening up possibilities for major structural change. Librarians as experts on information and information use need to be aware of these relationships. We can use them to argue for a more central role for ourselves.

---

[10] See the discussion of “Information Technology and Organizational Structure”.

[11] See the discussions of “Core Competencies” and “Hierarchies to Markets”.

[12] See discussion on “Data Driven System Design”.

Key Articles:

Davenport, Thomas H. *Process Innovation: Reengineering Work through Information Technology*. Boston, Mass.: Harvard Business School Press, 1993.

Davenport, Thomas H. & Short, James E. "The New Industrial Engineering, Information Technology and Business Process Redesign." *Sloan Management Review* 31, no. 4 (1990): 11-27.

* *

HIERARCHIES TO MARKETS

The argument that constitutes the hierarchies and markets theme is a fascinating one due to the scope of its possible ramifications, both in the political sector as well as in economics and business. The basic precept is that an organization always faces a "make or buy" choice, and improved information and communication technology tends to continuously shift the balance point to the "buy" end of the balance.

Figure 6. Make or Buy Balance

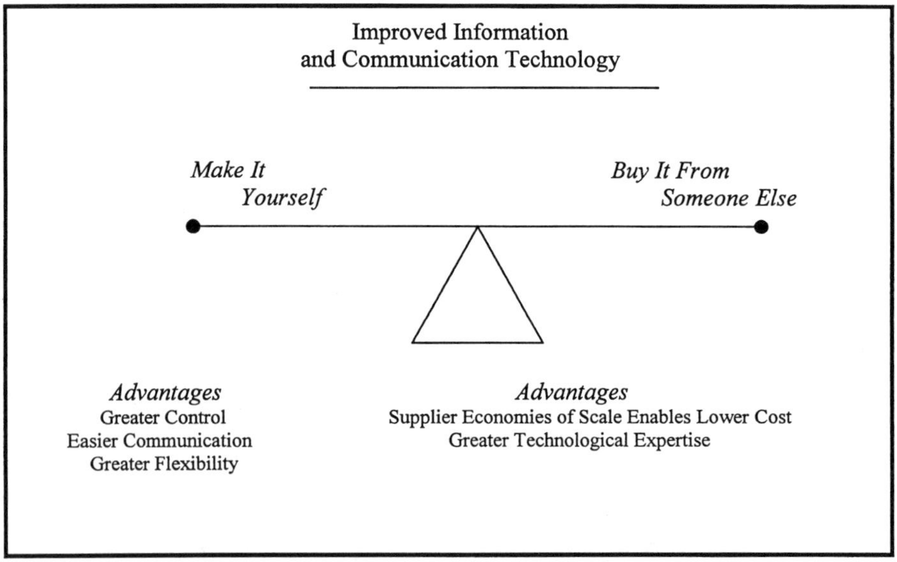

When making it oneself, one has greater and easier control. For example, it is easier to contact a division within your organization and request two hundred items for next Monday then it is to make a similar request with an outside supplier. However, an outside supplier who specializes in the particular product or technology[13] may be able, by virtue of economies of scale, to provide greater efficiency and lower prices, and to support more Research and Development, and thereby to offer a product that is closer to the state of the art and is qualitatively superior. Consider whether an automobile manufacturer should try to make their own batteries or buy them from a battery manufacturer who specializes in batteries for many applications, and who is likely to have spillover benefits from one application to another. The thesis is that improved information technology and communication makes it easier to establish real time and promptly responsive relations with suppliers. This erodes the advantage of making it yourself and pushes the advantage toward buying from specialist suppliers.

One ramification of the hierarchies to markets theme is that we will be seeing more and more specialized organizations, and less vertical integration. Vertical integration is the trend to do everything necessary to generate the end product, for example the automobile company that owned its own iron ore mining operations and its own rubber plantations to produce rubber

[13] See discussion under "Core Competencies".

for its automobile tires. The ultimate extension of this trend to specialization would be the "virtual company" in which a "company" is a continually changing and unfixed conglomeration of whatever units or individuals are needed at a particular time.

In one sense, the "hierarchies to markets" notion is another facet of the same larger phenomenon of which "core competencies" and "supply chain management" are other aspects.[14] Another major ramification making this particular facet fascinating, is that the same logic asserts that more effective decisions can be made at the local level because improved information and communications technology make it easier to move information. From this can be derived the propositions:

- central planning is an adaptive strategy for an information-sparse and communication-sparse environment,
- yet information technology is increasingly capable of putting more information into the hands of the people who can effectively use it in a more timely fashion and,
- in an information plentiful environment a market economy can respond faster and more effectively, and that advantage increases with the increasing capability of information technology.

This implies greater localization of decision making and a shift from central planning and hierarchies to market economies, greater competition, and more competitors. Airline deregulation and telecommunications deregulations are obvious components of this trend. Now we are beginning to see the deregulation of electric utilities. Indeed one can extend this thesis to the political dimensions and posit that the break-up of the centrally planned economic structure of the former Soviet Union was an inevitable consequence of this trend.

Ramifications for the Librarian

As one examines the evolution of librarianship in the last quarter century, one can see this progression in our own field. Increasingly we buy our cataloging rather than making it ourselves, and increasingly we buy database access from online hosts. How much further will we shift to the buy end of the spectrum? There is a tool here for thinking about the future of our field, as well as a way of examining your own company, predicting its possible evolution, and trying to stay ahead of events.

Key Articles:

Malone, Thomas W. and John F. Rockart. "Computers, Networks, and the Corporation." *Scientific American* 265, no. 3 (September 1991): 128-136.
Information technology moves operations from the 'make' to the 'buy' end of the spectrum.

Malone, Thomas W., Joanne Yates, and Robert I. Benjamin. "Electronic Markets and Electronic Hierarchies." *Communications of the ACM* 30, no. 6 (June 1987): 484-497.
Information technology moves economic activities from the hierarchical end to the market end of the spectrum.

[14] See discussions on "Core Competencies" and "Supply Chain Management".

* * *

COMPETITIVE INTELLIGENCE

The notion of competitive intelligence is not new, but it has enjoyed a resurgence of interest in the business community. This revival has been driven in large part by the increasing internationalization of business.[15] When the competition is not in the same country or the same continent it is difficult to be aware of what the competition may be intending. That in turn results in the need for a more conscious and explicit effort to stay on top of things and to acquire appropriate competitive intelligence. This is reinforced by the core competency thesis that implies the requirement to focus on the state of the art and remain equal with or ahead of competitors in your core competencies, with less reliance on natural markets. Similarly the hierarchies to markets phenomenon similarly implies less protection and market creation by government actions, more exposure to the vicissitudes of the market and competition, and consequently a greater need for competitive intelligence. Competitive intelligence overlaps to a considerable degree with environmental scanning.[16] This concept means deliberately attempting to consciously keep alert to trends in the environment, such as technology, legislation and regulation, and customer needs and expectations, that might effect the organization's success, create problems, or present opportunities.

Competitive Intelligence and the Librarian

Librarians are the experts on acquiring and organizing external information. Competitive intelligence is simply a tightly focused application of that expertise. There is no excuse for the librarian not playing a key role in competitive intelligence. It is no accident that in 1996 approximately forty percent of the membership of SCIP (the Society for Competitive Intelligence Professionals) were librarians.

Key Articles:

Classic Business Literature References:

Combs, R.E., and J.D. Moorehead. *The Competitive Intelligence Handbook.* Metuchen, NJ: Scarecrow, 1992.
Slim volume, good on techniques, not much about specific sources.

Tyson, K.W.M. *Competitor Intelligence Manual & Guide: Gathering, Analyzing and Using Business Intelligence.* Englewood Cliffs, NJ: Prentice Hall,1990.

Fuld, L.M. *Monitoring the Competition: Find out what's really going on over there.* New York: John Wiley & Sons, 1988.

Fuld, L.M. *Competitor Intelligence: How to get it-how to use it.* New York: John Wiley & Sons, 1985.

Sammon, W.L, M.A. Kurland, and R. Spitalnic. *Business Competitor Intelligence: Methods for Collecting, Organizing, and Using Information.* New York: John Wiley & Sons, 1984.

---

[15] See discussions about "Core Competencies" and "Hierarchies to Markets".
[16] See discussion on "MIS to DSS".

Note: the above are pre-Internet.

The principal journal in the field is:

Hohhof, B., ed. *Competitive Intelligence Review*. Washington, DC: Society of Competitive Intelligence Professionals, 1990-.

SCIP members automatically receive every issue of CIR. For nonmembers who wish to subscribe directly from the publisher, the annual price is $112 in the United States, $152 in Canada and Mexico, $174 outside North America. Subscription orders/inquires should be directed to John Wiley & Sons, Inc. at 212-850-6645 or E-mail: SUBINFO@jwiley.com.

Note: SCIP, the Society for Competitive Intelligence Professionals is an international society, with chapters and affiliates in Belgium, Canada, Germany, Italy, Mexico, South Africa, the United Kingdom and the USA.

SCIP (www.scip.org)
1700 Diagonal Rd. Suite 520
Alexandria, Virginia, 22314, USA
Tel: (703) 739-0696; Fax (703) 739-2524; E-mail: postmaster@scip.org

SCIP
Boulevard St. Michel 15
1040 Brussels, Belgium
Tel: +32-3-743-1543; Fax: +32-2-743-155; E-mail: 10332.670@compuserve.com

Library Literature:

A special issue of *Library Trends* 43, no. 2 (Fall 1994): 149-287, is devoted to "The library in Corporate Intelligence activities". Copies of this issue available for $18.50, including postage. Order from the University of Illinois Press, Journals Department, 1325 S. Oak St., Champaign, IL 61820, Telephone 217-333-8935, MasterCard and Visa are accepted.

Particularly salient articles are:

Auster, Ethel, and Chun Wei Choo. "CEOs, Information, and Decision Making: Scanning the Environment for Strategic Advantage." *Library Trends* 43, no. 2 (Fall 1994): 206-225.

Hohhof, Bonnie. "Developing Information Systems for Competitive Intelligence Support." *Library Trends* 43, no. 2 (Fall 1994): 226-230.

Walker, Thomas D. "The Literature of Competitive Intelligence." *Library Trends* 43, no. 2 (Fall 1994): 271-284.
A good analysis of the literature and key journals.

Other articles:

Choo, Chun Wei, and Ethel Auster. "Environmental Scanning: Acquisition and Use of Information by Managers. In *Annual Review of Information Science and Technology* v. 28: 279-314, Martha E. Williams, ed. Medford, NJ: Learned Information, 1993.

Auster, Ethel, and Chun Wei Choo. "How Senior Managers Acquire and Use Information in Environmental Scanning." *Information Processing & Management* 30, no. 5 (1994): 607-618

*

TQM AND BENCHMARKING

It would be difficult to write about business fads and management concepts of the 1980s and 1990s without mentioning TQM, Total Quality Management. Actually TQM is not an information driven concept in the sense that we have in mind here. There are two basic concepts behind TQM. The most basic thrust is quality control and in particular enlarging the responsibility for quality control from engineers and quality control staff to include the operators on the floor. The second is precisely that of the employee involvement and the ramifications of greater involvement, not only in the quality control of the process as it exists at any particular time, but also in the role of improving the processes and the products. These basic elements are information driven only in the sense of statistical quality control (not really relevant to the thrust of this document), and in the sense of better and more creative information flow within the organization, an important concept that reappears with a new name as Knowledge Management.

TQM, based on the work of Deming, was in fact not all that new. It first appeared, at least among the developed countries of the North Atlantic, in the 1960s when it was known as "zero defects". The enthusiasm waned however, at least partly because in the hot economies of the 1960s business felt no great impetus to change (if it ain't broke, don't fix it), but with the economic slow down of the late 1970s, and the increasing internationalization of competition, by the 1980s the world was ready for the gospel of TQM.

When zero defects reappeared as TQM, two new items were added to the gospel. The first was a focus on servicing the customer, but not only with better quality more defect free products, but also with improved attention to quality and timeliness of service and with increased attention to what the customers real needs were. The second was the notion of benchmarking. Benchmarking is the process of examining any process your organization performs, finding out who else needs to undertake that same process (whether in your industry or not), then finding out who performs it best, and then using their performance as a benchmark against which to compare your own performance, and with which to generate new expectations and standards about what constitutes first class performance, and to generate new ideas about how to improve your performance.

The Librarian and Benchmarking

While the general ideas of TQM are applicable to almost any operation, including the library itself, it is the process of benchmarking that is information driven and that provides a lever for the librarian. General management of any organization is likely to know a good bit about the competition and how they go about things, and they are likely to have the contacts to gather more information. The notion of benchmarking however is broader than just keeping track of your competition and how they do things. Benchmarking means an analysis by function and process. If order fulfillment is an important part of your organizations operations, then benchmarking implies that you do not just find out how your competitors handle order fulfillment, but that you find out how order fulfillment is handled in entirely unrelated industries. Where is it done well? What can we learn? What can we import? How can we steal a march on our competitors and create a competitive advantage?

Here, the librarians search skills and expertise with the literature outside the industry is a real advantage. Who better than the librarian, the trained searcher, for playing the key role in bringing knowledge of how things are handled outside the industry into the organization? Bringing such knowledge into the organization is one of the classic functions of the management consultant. The librarian can point out that they can provide much the same sort of knowledge at a much lower cost, and that at the very least, they can complement the expertise of the consultant. To do this effectively however, the librarian must be proactive and not wait for the request to come to them. The librarian has to either attach themselves to the TQM or benchmarking team, or go do it unbidden, and then present what has been found to the appropriate executive.

* * *

INFORMATION TECHNOLOGY AND PRODUCTIVITY

A key driver of modern business thinking is that the appropriate use of information technology (IT) enhances productivity. A good example of this increased productivity is modern communications, such as telephony and email, which rely on highly sophisticated electronic switches to make connections instead of the manual method used by early telephone operators. Imagine the personnel that would need to be employed if connections had to be made by operators plugging cables in and out of switchboards. This seems so obvious that it hardly seems worth debating.

In the late 1980s however there was a strong reaction to this conventional wisdom, and the phrase "productivity paradox" was coined to describe the phenomenon that despite increasing expenditures on IT, productivity figures, calculated in the conventional fashion, did not seem to be rising. If the thesis about IT and productivity was true, and if more was being spent on IT, then why were productivity figures not rising? --the productivity paradox.

Assertions of the existence of the productivity paradox brought a number of responses. The most obvious response was simply that there are many intangible or at least functionally intangible benefits that are not measured by productivity calculations. What is the utility of higher definition television, or of a vastly increased number of channels? The second response is that there are many benefits that could, at least in principle, be measured but are not. A good example of this is the productivity of the pharmaceutical industry. Suppose there were no Chemical Abstracts or Beilstein outline, no structure-activity-relationship software, no substructure searching, no synthetic chemical pathway analysis, no receptor-site modeling, no "rational drug design." It is quite reasonable to postulate that we might well be at least half a decade or so behind where we are now in the development of effective new therapeutic agents. But, would the productivity calculations for the pharmaceutical industry look any different? Probably not, pharmaceutical industry sales would not differ markedly from those at present; consumers would simply be buying less effective therapeutic agents. However, the conventional productivity calculations make no provision for the efficacy of therapeutic agents, much less for issues, such as extension of life expectancy or increases in the quality of life.

Similarly the point is made that for financial services, the productivity calculations take no notice of the quality of service to the consumer, or of productivity and efficiency as perceived by the consumer. Certainly few of us would wish to return to a world with no ATMs, automated teller machines, no automated banking centers at the airport. Yet, the productivity calculations for the financial services industry behave (are calculated) as though this dramatic improvement in customer service and system productivity had never taken place.[17] We could attempt to measure many of these things, but we do not.

A third response is that many of the capabilities and outputs of information technology are used simply to gain or maintain competitive advantage, that competitive advantage is often a sponge soaking up the benefits of information technology. Loveman provides the example of the airline industry, where immense information technology resources are utilized to support frequent flyer programs and an enormously Byzantine fare structure, with little discernible overall effect on productivity.[18] Inherent in the nature of information is the capability for it to

[17] H. Banks, "The Productivity Paradox," *Forbes* 144, no. 2 (1989): 15.
[18] G. Loveman, "Cash Drain, No Gain," *Computerworld* 25, no. 47 (1991): 69-72.

be modified and varied to a degree far in excess of what is achievable with more concrete conventional goods. It is therefore not surprising that a large component of information technology costs seem to be consumed for the purposes of creating product differentiation without enhancing productivity. That may just be the inevitable nature of the beast.

Another response, perhaps the most compelling, is the argument that our present calculations of productivity in the service sector are hopelessly flawed. The argument is that as our economics become increasingly service industry based, productivity calculations will inevitably and meaninglessly converge, because the measure of output is simply the amount paid for service. Both the cost of providing services and the amount paid for services will asymptotically converge on the amount of total wages paid. The ratio of two numbers converging on the same thing (the amount paid for the service divided by the cost of providing services) will inevitably converge on unity; anything divided by itself is one. Thus it can be argued that the standard measure of productivity in a service environment is fundamentally doomed to be increasingly meaningless and that to have meaningful measures we must totally overhaul how the productivity of services is calculated.

A final argument is that it simply is too soon to see such an effect. David shows a fascinating parallel to the introduction of electric power and the electric motor, and reveals how surprisingly long it took for that technology to have a measurable impact on industrial productivity.[19] Indeed, Koenig and Wilson link the David thesis with the enthusiasm for BPR (Business Process Reengineering)[20] and draw the analogies:

print-on-paper
- is to -
business process redesign   as   shafts, pulleys, and belts
- are to -
manufacturing process redesign

and

business process reengineering
- is to -
the computer and information technology   as   manufacturing process redesign
- is to -
the dynamo and electrical technology

They point out that at almost precisely the same time that the literature revealed concern about the productivity paradox, the notion of business process reengineering appeared. The reason that David posits that the dynamo and the grid took so long to have an effect was that major industrial redesign, manufacturing process redesign, had to be accomplished first. New factories that were not built around pulleys and shafts, factories that were built to take advantage of unit drive capability (machines that were driven directly by an electric motor, rather than connected to a central mechanical power source) had to be constructed before a dramatic effect was seen. If this thesis is correct, that business process redesign is the factory rebuilding of the computer age, then we are about to enter an era of noticeably improved productivity.

In summary, the conventional wisdom has become that the productivity paradox is more apparent than real. Some IT capability does get "squandered" on things that enhance or bolster an organization's competitive position but that do not increase productivity in any meaningful sense. The principle explanation however, lies in our inability to measure productivity, particularly in service industries, and particularly for those services that are

---

[19] P.A. David, "The Dynamo and the Computer," *American Economic Review* 80, no. 2 (1990): 355-361.

[20] See discussion on "Business Process Reengineering".

most likely to be enhanced or made more productive by the more sophisticated use of information and information technology.

The Librarian and Information Technology and Productivity

For the librarian the thesis of the central role of information and information technology in terms of enhancing productivity is an argument to conjure with. But, the librarian must, if that thesis is to be used effectively, be able to discuss the so-called productivity paradox and be able to discount it effectively. The librarian should also be able to make the case that library services enhance productivity, but it is beyond the scope of this piece to review that literature, but references to the key pieces are included below.

Key Articles:

General:

Articles and books about libraries and librarianship and their effect in Organizational Productivity:

Koenig, M.E.D. "Information Services and Downstream Productivity." In *The Annual Review of Information Science and Technology* v. 25: 55-86. Martha E. Williams, ed. New York: Elsevier, 1990.
Best overall review of the subject.

Koenig, M.E.D. "The Importance of Information Services for Productivity Under-recognized and Under-invested." *Special Libraries* 83, no. 4 (Fall 1992): 199-210.
A distillation of the above.

Griffiths, Jose-Marie, and Donald W. King. *Special Libraries: Increasing the Information Edge*. Washington, D.C.: Special Libraries Association, 1993.
An excellent summary of the extensive work of King and Griffiths in quantifying the impact of libraries and information centers.

Koenig, M.E.D. "The Information Environment and the Productivity of Research." In *Recent Advances in Chemical Information*, H.Collier, ed. London: Royal Society of Chemistry, 1992, 133-143.
This is probably the most robust study on the impact of libraries upon productivity. Reprinted in the following work.

Grimshaw, Anne., ed. *Information Culture and Business Performance*. Information Strategy Report 2, prepared for the British Library by Hertis Information and Research. Hatfield, Hertfordshire, U.K.: University of Hertfordshire Press, 1995.
This is another very good overview of the subject.

Marshall, Joanne G. " The Impact of the Hospital Library on Clinical Decision Making: The Rochester Study." *Bulletin of the Medical Library Association* 80, no. 2 (April 1992): 169-178.
An excellent study; from it can be derived the argument that better library service not only results in better patient care, but also reduced cost.

King, D.N. "The Contribution of Hospital Library Services to Clinical Care: A Study in eight hospitals." *Bulletin of the Medical Library Association* 75, no. 4, (1987): 291-301.

Marshall, Joanne G. *The Impact of the Special Library in Corporate Decision Making*. Washington, D.C.: Special Libraries Association, 1993.
Both are good cases reporting the positive impact of libraries on organizational effectiveness.

Other Productivity Paradox Articles:

David, P.A. "The Dynamo and the Computer: An Historical Perspective on the Modern Productivity Paradox." *American Economic Review* 80, no. 2 (1990): 355-361.

Koenig, M.E.D., and Thomas D. Wilson. "Productivity Growth, The Take-Off Point." *Information Processing and Management* 32, no. 2 (1996): 247-254.

The articles one needs to be able to debunk:

Loveman, G. "Cash Drain, No Gain." *Computerworld* 25, no. 47 (1991): 69-72.

Banks, H. "The Productivity Paradox." *Forbes* 144, no. 2 (1989): 15.

Roach, S.S. "Services Under Siege-the Restructuring Imperative." *Harvard Business Review* 69, no. 5 (1991): 82-91.

*

MINIMIZATION OF UNALLOCATED COST

The concept of minimization of unallocated cost is based on the distinction between two types of cost incurred by an organization. First, there are those costs that are directly attributable or allocatable to the organization's output. Second, there are those costs which are not attributable and which must be treated as overhead, also known as burden, or general and administrative (g & a) costs. Basic accounting doctrine holds that the smaller the proportion of unattributable cost the better the decision-making performance of the organization.

The logic behind this management principal is straightforward and persuasive. For example, any organization has inputs and outputs. It acquires inputs, typically through purchases and gifts, and then processes those inputs in some fashion. Finally, it produces outputs such as educated students or retrospective searches. If an organization is to be competitive – if it is to perform well – it must determine what business it is in and what outputs it should produce. The phrase enterprise analysis has been coined for this process. (See the section on Enterprise-Wide Information Analysis.) The organization must also determine what inputs are needed and how to efficiently and effectively process those inputs to produce the desired outputs.

An important component of determining appropriate outputs and a central component of determining efficiency is linking the inputs to the outputs, i.e., the process of allocation (or apportionment in British English). And, the greater the number of unallocated costs, the poorer the linkage between inputs and outputs. Just like unsprung weight in a racecar, unallocated cost is to be minimized. The more that costs can be allocated to outputs – assuming a reasonably justifiable allocation scheme – and, therefore, the fewer the unallocated costs, then the better the decision-making process and the performance of the organization should be.

Unallocated Cost and the Librarian

The implications for librarians are obvious - the more important, and the more expensive, libraries and information centers become, the less management can afford to treat them as overhead items, and the more libraries and information centers will be asked to account for and allocate their costs. Librarians are generally more comfortable thinking of their service as a public good, not as a service that needs to be carefully allocated to the program, product or constituency supported. Librarians will have to increasingly undertake such allocations or apportionment. It is in general better to approach the need proactively than to wait until a management directive arrives. The most salient point is that approaching the trend proactively gives the librarian a better chance to organize a process in which the allocation is done annually at budget time at the departmental or unit level, without the user seeing a direct change. If the librarian waits to respond reactively, it is likely to be much more difficult to fend off ill-conceived proposals to charge directly for library or information service, a solution that is likely to be counter-productive. This theme and its ramifications are discussed at some length in the article by Koenig. Within the business literature, the most salient article is by Dearden in the *Harvard Business Review*.

Key Articles:

Koenig, M.E.D. "Fiscal Accountability, and the Principle of Minimum Unsprung Weight." *The Bottom Line* 1, no. 1 (1987): 18-22.

Dearden, John. "Cost Accounting Comes to Service Industries." *Harvard Business Review* 56, no. 5 (September-October 1978): 132-140.

* * *

INFORMATION TECHNOLOGY AND ORGANIZATIONAL STRUCTURE

For several decades, there has been much speculation about the effect of information technology on the structure of organizations. Thomas Whisler did the seminal research and predicted that organizations would become flatter with fewer, particularly mid-level professional jobs.[21] Such generalizations, however, have fallen into disfavor. Numerous counter examples have been found, for example, the insurance industry where Brophy points out that the effect of information technology has been to markedly increase the ration of professional to non-professional staff.[22]

The central theme that has emerged is that we have been far too unaware of how much the structure of organization and bureaucracies has been shaped by the limitation of print-on-paper and the requirement to shape job and functional unit parameters around the availability of information. Information technology, however, is increasingly providing the capability to place the information where the user is[23], rather than require the user to go or be where the information is, and some of the resulting reconfigurations can be quite dramatic. Current thinking therefore is that while the effects of information technology are often dramatic they are very context specific, and very difficult to categorize and predict, and thus for a variety of reasons demand management attention.

IT and Organizational Structure and Business Process Reengineering, although the link is seldom explicitly acknowledged, both stem from the shared realization that the structure of many organizations is deeply influenced and severely limited by the constraints of print-on-paper technology. In the past, these constraints were either taken for granted or went unnoticed. Electronic information systems liberates systems design and enables structures that are quite different from how things were organized in the past.

> ***Information Technology and Organizational Structure*** is the passive viewpoint - the awareness that now IT systems will bring with them major changes in organizational structure, and such changes require senior management attention.
>
> ***Business Process Reengineering*** is the active viewpoint - the argument that the new capabilities of IT allow us to design simpler, more effective, more productive organizational structures than were possible in the era of print-on-paper technology, and we should proactively pursue those opportunities.

Changes in organizational structure tend to be very threatening to many people. Revisions in organizational structure alter job domains, create new job domains, and eliminate jobs. Since in a modern society we tend to define oneself by our job domain, such changes are highly charged, and demand top management attention and planning.

One good example of such effects is that of The Travelers insurance company, headquartered in Hartford, Connecticut. They estimate that in the decade from the mid 1980s to the mid

[21] Thomas L. Whisler. *Information Technology and Organizational Change,* Belmont, California: Wadsworth Publishing Company, 1970.

[22] Joseph T. Brophy. Presentation at the Conference Board's 3rd Annual Conference on New Opportunites in Management Information, New York: April 17-18, 1985.

[23] Kenn and Barrow. Complete citation follows this discussion.

1990s their business tripled in volume, and the number of employee's remained relatively stable at around 30,000. However, the composition of that employment changed dramatically from roughly 10,000 professionals and 20,000 clerical to roughly 20,000 professionals and 10,000 clerical. This shift was due almost entirely to improved IT and the delivery of information online to the agent in his of her office that formerly would have had to be accessed by a file clerk at the head office in Hartford. At one level this constitutes a wonderful change, 10,000 jobs have been upgraded from clerical to professional. At another level it has been a devastating change for Hartford Connecticut where thousands of jobs have disappeared. True, new jobs have been created, but they are in Illinois or Brazil, not much help to the jobless in Hartford. Such modifications require understanding, planning, and they obviously demand top management involvement not merely oversight.[24]

At a larger level, and in some ways even more compelling, is the realization that information technology can reshape not only individual organizations but the whole structure of industries, and thus also change the nature of competition and the boundaries of organizations. One example of such a change is the introduction of Electronic Data Interchange (EDI) between consumer and supplier. EDI is closely linked with JIT, "Just In Time", inventory and production management. The consequences of information technology is that EDI and JIT can link the manufacturer directly with the producers of the components used and this has the potential to eliminate various levels of middle-men, such as wholesalers, and jobbers. This has already happened to a considerable degree in the automobile after market, and in health care products.

A further extension of the argument is that improved information technology will lead to less vertical integration in the industry.[25] This is really the micro-economic version of the thesis that information technology is moving economic activity from central planning to market driven systems.[26] Making things within the organization minimizes coordination costs, but reduces choice and the ability to take advantage of the specialist economics of scale. Improved information technology reduces communication and coordination costs and therefore shifts the balance toward the buy end of the make versus buy spectrum, and leads to more specialization. Articles on the importance of "core competencies" for an organization can be viewed as another aspect of that same phenomenon, a convergence on the conclusion about specialization, but arriving there without even touching upon information technology.[27]

Information Technology and Organizational Structure and the Librarian

The salient point for librarians and information officers is the argument that information systems planning must involve senior management.

Key Articles:

Davis, Stan and Jim Botkin. "The Coming of Knowledge-Based Business." *Harvard Business Review* 72, no. 5 (September/October, 1994): 165-170.

---

[24] This is a good example of what Gibson and Jackson have in mind in their "transformation stage". See discussion on "Information System Stage Hypothesis".

[25] Malone and Rockart, and Huber. Complete citations follows this discussion.

[26] See section on "Hierarchies to Markets".

[27] Prahalad and Hamel. Complete citation follows this discussion. See also the discussion on "Core Competencies".

Johnston, Russel, and Paul R. Lawrence. "Beyond Vertical Integration – The Rise of the Value Adding Partnership." *Harvard Business Review* 66, no. 4 (July/August, 1988): 94-101.

See also:

Barrow, Craig. "Implementing an Executive Information System: Seven Steps for Success." *Journal of Information Systems Management* 7, no. 2 (1990): 41-46.

Brophy, Joseph T. Presentation at the Conference Board's 3rd Annual Conference on New Opportunities in Management Information. New York: April 17-18, 1985.

Gibson, Cyrus F., and Barbara Bund Jackson. *The Information Imperative: Managing the Impact of Information Technology on Business and People.* Lexington, Mass.: D.C. Heath, 1987.

Huber, Peter. "The Unbundling of America." *Forbes* 149, no. 8 (April 13, 1992): 118.

Keen, Peter G.W. "Information Systems and Organizational Change." *Communications of the ACM* 24, no. 1 (1981): 24-33.
Classic article on the impact of and resistance to changes caused by new information systems.

Malone, Thomas W., and John F. Rockart. "Computers, Networks, and the Corporation." *Scientific American* 265, no. 3 (September 1991): 128-136.
Information technology moves operations from the 'make' to the 'buy' end of the spectrum.

Malone, Thomas W., Joanne Yates, and Robert I. Benjamin, "Electronic Markets and Electronic Markets and Electronic Hierarchies." *Communications of the ACM* 30, no. 6 (June 1987): 484-497.
Information technology moves economic activities from the hierarchical end to the market end of the spectrum.

Prahalad C.K., and Gary Hamel. "The Core Competence of the Corporation." *Harvard Business Review* 68, no. 3 (May/June, 1990): 79-91.
The seminal article on core competencies.

Whisler, Thomas L. *Information Technology and Organizational Change.* Belmont, California: Wadsworth Publishing Company, 1970.
The seminal piece for this field; although now outdated is important for historical reasons.

* *

INFORMATION RESOURCE MANAGEMENT

Information Resource Management (IRM) is a term that is now rather dated and has been replaced by the term "Knowledge Management" previously discussed. The librarian should however be cognizant of the term, and its history. IRM arose in the 1970s, and was to an extent an offspring of the enthusiasm for MIS systems, discussed in a subsequent section. It was basically the recognition that information was a resource that the organization should explicitly pay attention to and manage, just as it managed finance, inventory, or personnel. The concept received additional momentum when in the paperwork reduction act of 1980; US government agencies were required to assign a senior manager the responsibility of information management. This person was to look holistically at how the agency was using information, how it was making information available, and was to develop appropriate polices. The impact of the act was not what it might have been, the agency was not required to appoint a full time information resource manager, and the requirement was typically treated simply as an added collateral duty for some existing post. Nonetheless, it did focus attention of the premise that information was important, that it was a resource, and that explicit senior management attention should be paid to it. What has happened recently, is that in essence the notion, after a decade and a half of relative quiescence, has exploded in popularity and became known as "knowledge management". Knowledge management is typically perceived as a hot new concept, but it has its roots in the concept of IRM.

Key Articles:

Three good review articles:

Bergeron, Pierette. "Information Resources Management." In *Annual Review of Information Science and Technology* v. 31: 263-300, Martha E. Williams, ed. Medford, NJ: Information Today, for the American Society for Information Science, 1996.

Lytle, Richard H. "Information Resources Management: 1981-1986." In *Annual Review of Information Science and Technology* v. 21: 309-336, Martha E. Williams, ed. White Plains, NY: Knowledge Industry Publications, Inc. for the American Society of Information Science, 1982.

Levitan, Karen B. "Information Resource(s) Management - IRM. In *Annual Review of Information Science and Technology* v. 17: 227-266, Martha E. Williams, ed. White Plains, NY: Knowledge Industry Publications, Inc. for the American Society for Information Science, 1982.

The best known overview in the business tradition:

Synnott, William R., and William H. Gruber. *Information Resource Management: Opportunities and Strategies for the 1980s*. New York, NY: Wiley, 1981.

Scott Morton, Michael S., ed. *The Corporation of the 1990s: Information Technology and Organizational Transformation*. New York, NY: Oxford University Press, 1991.

Other useful background pieces:

Boaden, Ruth, and Geoff Lockett. "Information Technology, Information Systems, and Information Management: Definition and Development." *European Journal of Information Systems* 1, no. 1 (1991): 23-32.

Broadbent, Marianne, and Michael E. D. Koenig. "Information and Information Technology Management." In *Annual Review of Information and Science Technology* v. 23: 237-270, Martha E. Williams, ed. Amsterdam, The Netherlands: Elsevier Science Publishers for the American Society for Information Science, 1988.

Burk, Cornelius F., and Forest W. Horton Jr. *InfoMap: A Complete Guide to Discovering Corporate Information Resources*. Englewood Cliffs, NJ: Prentice-Hall, 1988.

Marchand, Donald A. "Information Management: Strategies and Tools in Transition." *Information Management Review* 1 (1985): 27-37.

* * *

ENTERPRISE-WIDE INFORMATION ANALYSIS

Enterprise Wide Information Analysis is a phrase coined by IBM (International Business Machines) in the early 1980s. The basic idea is very simple, and very elegant, but it needs to be put in a contextual setting by way of background. IBM had for some years run free courses for its customers on what it called 'business systems planning', or planning for how much data processing capability an organization would need in the future. IBM had developed a rather detailed and quite useful approach to something that is as much art as science. IBM was not offering their free courses altruistically. If data processing managers could plan better and make a more convincing case to management as to what resources would be necessary in the future, then those plans and eventual purchases would be more likely to be approved, and IBM would generate greater sales and receive revenue earlier.

In the late 1970s the phrase "critical success factors" had become very popular to describe the concept that management should not merely respond to current issues and emergencies, crisis management, but should take the time to carefully analyze what factors were critical to the success of the organization. The analysis would examine what proportion of the organization's responses and management attention was being diverted toward what ends and in particular toward those critical factors, and was there a reasonable match, and if not, why not? Were the critical factors receiving the attention, both in terms of resources and of management attentions that was warranted?

Critical Success Factors is at one level very obvious and unremarkable. Of course you should pay attention to what is critical. The utility of the phrase is to make that advice succinct, to give it a name, and to suggest the exercise and the discipline of frequently examining whether your resources are indeed going to critical areas or whether they are dissipated elsewhere.

Enterprise Wide Information Analysis is basically the grafting of the critical success factors notion onto business systems planning. The basic precepts of Enterprise Wide Information Analysis are:

1. Determine what your <u>Enterprise</u> is.
2. Determine what <u>Decisions</u> have to be made correctly to be successful in that enterprise.
3. Determine what <u>Information</u> is needed to make those decisions correctly.

Then from the above, proceed with your business systems planning and decide what IT capabilities will be required. The attractiveness to IBM of the incorporation of critical success factors into the articulation of Enterprise Wide Information Analysis was the steps above that were added on top of business systems planning, particularly points one and two. These two issues demanded the attention and the participation of top management, not only the head of data processing. This necessarily brought BSP, now called EWIA to the attention of top management, which was all to the benefit of IBM. A basic precept in marketing is to make your pitch as high in the organization as possible, and the more top management was aware of future IT needs, the more likely IBM was to get revenue sooner.

Enterprise Wide Information Analysis and the Librarian

The importance of Enterprise Wide Information Analysis to the librarian is the elegance and the persuasiveness of the fashion in which it highlights the importance of information and its utilization and application to the organization. The very platitudinousness and obviousness of critical success factors becomes its strength in Enterprise Wide Information Analysis. Who can argue with the three steps previously mentioned? The organization, specifically its management, must decide what the organization is about, what exactly the enterprise is and what it is trying to accomplish. Given that, management must make the appropriate decisions correctly, who can argue with the point that this is management's key role, to select the appropriate decisions to be made and to make them correctly? If this is to be accomplished, one needs the right information. Enter the librarian/information officer. We librarians should be embarrassed that we did not originate and popularize the concept.

Key Articles:

Parker, M.M. "Enterprise Information Analysis: Cost Benefit Analysis and Data Managed System." *IBM Systems Journal* 21, no. 1 (1982): 108-123.

Parker, M.M. *Enterprise-Wide Information Management: Emerging Information Requirements*. Los Angeles, California: IBM Corporation, 1985.

* *

MIS TO DSS, AND EXTERNAL INFORMATION

In the 1970s there was a great enthusiasm for what were then termed management information systems (MIS). As data processing systems developed, the awareness grew that most organizations had large amounts of data and information contained in electronic form. The problem was that the data and information was scattered in various systems, often incompatible systems, throughout the organization, and the information could only be accessed in a local and piecemeal fashion, not in an integrated fashion. At the same time, database management systems (DBMSs) were appearing on the market. DBMSs were designed to serve as one central data repository for an organization and yet allow application programs to access it independently and allow each application systems to appear to each user as a specific information system with its own specific data store. The concept then arose that management could access this central data store to address and support management decision making.

After much enthusiasm for MIS development, a backlash of disappointment occurred when it became apparent that MIS systems were not performing as advertised, and that executives were not using them to any great extent. The classic expression of the disappointment was Russell Ackoff's article, "Management Mis-Information Systems".

Gradually it became clear that the principle reason for the shortcomings of MISs was that they contained, for the most part, the wrong information. If one thinks of the classic representation of organizational decision making as a pyramid with day to day shop floor level decision making at the bottom of the pyramid, and long range planning and strategic executive decision making at the top, then the problem becomes apparent.

Figure 7. Management Decision Making and the Information Frame

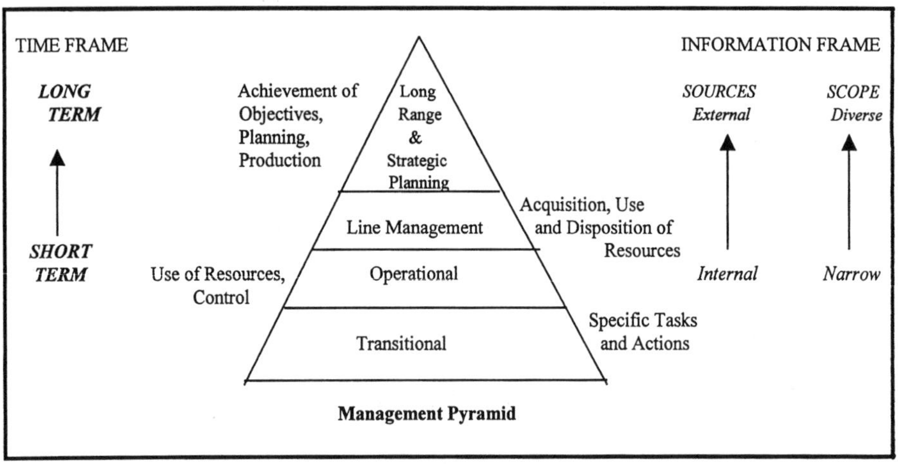

The MIS systems were aggregations of the organization's internal transaction data, what was received, what was produced, what was shipped, etc. That internal data and information is precisely what is used for day-to-day ship floor management, but as one goes up the management triangle, external information becomes more and more important, and as we reach the apex of the pyramid, it becomes predominant. What is the expected rate of growth of such and such an industry? What are the competitor's capabilities? How rapidly will such and such a technology emerge?

In short, MIS systems, which had been trumpeted as systems for senior management, had the wrong information, almost exclusively internal information and minimal external information. The result of this disenchantment with MISs was, among other things, to increase the recognition of the importance of external information for high level decision making. For librarians, who specialize in the provision of and access to external information, this was a key development.

The basic MIS idea, to make information available to senior level management is a sound one, so the idea did not die, it reemerged with a new name, decision support systems (DSS). The principle changes were improvements in ease of use, not entirely coincidentally this coincided with major development in graphical user interfaces (GUIs), and the provision of more information, particularly external information. In recent years, a related buzzword has evolved, "environmental scanning", which refers to keeping abreast of what is happening and is likely to happen in your organization's domain of operations. Environmental scanning implies a structured organized approach with the assistance of some automated mechanism. This is similar to what librarians have long practiced and provided current awareness services and SDI (Selective Dissemination of Information), current awareness provided with the help of an electronic database. Again, not entirely coincidentally, the emphasis on environmental scanning coincided with the arrival of Lotus Notes and application packages, such as Hoover that used Lotus Notes to provide an SDI service to the desktop.

Importance for Librarians

The key point for librarians is the recognition of the importance of external information for executive decision making. Librarians need to increase the awareness of the fact that they are the experts on external information, locating it, organizing it, and providing it. Librarians need to take an organic stance in using IT, particularly corporate Intranets, in providing information. In Particular we need to take the lead in organizing and managing the information on our organization's Intranets.[28]

Key Articles:

Ackoff, Russell L. "Management Misinformation Systems." *Management Science* 14, no. 4 (1967): 147-156.

Dearden, John. "MIS Is a Mirage" *Harvard Business Review* 50, no. 1 (1972): 90-99.

Caldwell, Bruce. "The Answer are Blowing' in the Wind." *Information Week* (Cover Story) 417 (March 22 1993): 35-39.

[28] Observe how nicely this emphasis on external information complements the concept of enterprise wide information analysis.

* * *

INFORMATION TECHNOLOGY AS COMPETITIVE ADVANTAGE

The potential role of information technology in securing competitive advantage for an organization was probably the hottest topic in the entire business literature in the 1980s, and it remains an important theme. The thrust of the argument was that information technology, IT, when skillfully employed could in various ways differentiate an organization from its competition, add value to its services or products in the eyes of the customers, and secure a competitive advantage in comparison to the competition. The key point was that this thesis explicitly said that IT was no longer a backroom support function that could be left to mid level management to implement in their individual realms. Rather, IT was a major strategic enabler that could secure competitive advantage and affect the success and the very survival of the firm. As such, it demanded top level attention. IT could no longer be left to mid level management. This thesis thrust the employment of information, information technology and the design of information systems into an entirely new light, and assigned to them an importance that they had never had before.

The classic example of the use of IT to gain competitive advantage, cited often in the early literature in the field was the example of American Hospital Supply, a distributor of medical supplies to hospitals, clinics, pharmacies, etc. American Hospital Supply (AHS) distributed very good inventory control software to its major customers, and where needed helped with the acquisition of robust PCs, personal computers. Good inventory management is of course of great importance in the distribution of medical supplies. Then, when the customers were happily using the software, AHS distributed software enhancements and where necessary modems. When the inventory control software indicated that it was time to reorder an item, the order could, with no more effort than a keystroke or two, be electronically transmitted to AHS with receipt acknowledged electronically and shipment confirmed electronically (with print-on-paper backup and reports printed as needed). In short, items could be ordered, confirmed, and shipment particulars received not only much more promptly, but also much more easily and at less expense to the customers than by ordering from a competitor. While competitors scrambled to catch up, AHS increased its market share in North America from thirteen percent to nearly thirty percent.

The example illustrates both of the two key and most written about tactics of using IT for securing competitive advantage.

- Creating an added value to your goods and resources that is advantageous and that your competitor does not offer.
- Using IT to establish a linkage, a shared method of operation between your organization and your customer(s) that
    1. Makes it difficult for a competitor to enter the market - that is, it creates a barrier to market entry, and
    2. Makes it difficult (and expensive) for your customers to change suppliers.

The third theme in the competitive advantage literature is simply that of using information technology smartly to lower your costs of operation and thereby gain an advantage on your competitors.

The IT and competitive advantage thesis became so popular that there was inevitably a bit of a pendulum swing back. Hopper argued in his "Rattling Sabre" article that the advantage gained by IT was generally temporary, and as information systems development became more modular, more networked, and more platform independent, the period in which an organization enjoyed a competitive advantage before its competitors countered its advantage would become briefer. Even at face value though, Hopper's arguments mean only that your advantage is not permanent, but no one anticipates permanence in the highly competitive would of modern business. Furthermore, an American Airlines passenger reservation system, Sabre, in many years has generated more profit through its use by other airlines and by travel agents, than has American's aircraft operations. The Sabre System was also cited as an example of IT as competitive advantage. American Airlines was charged by other airlines with profiting unfairly by having its systems present flight options not in a neutral fashion, but with its own flights unfairly emphasized.[29] Therefore Hopper, who was the architect of Sabre, had a real motivation to argue that the advantage was not so much as had been hyped.

In any case, there remains a strong awareness that IT will have to be employed smartly merely to remain competitive. If an organization intends to edge ahead of or to outflank its competitors it is very likely that its strategy will emphasize or at least employ the strategic use of information and information technology. From the vantagepoint of libraries, the consequence is the imperative placed upon information and IT, and the perception that the employment of information and IT must engage the attention of senior management.

Key Articles:

Gerstein, M., and H. Reisman. "Creating Competitive Advantage with Computer Technology." *Journal of Business Strategy* 3, no. 1 (1982): 53-60.

Parsons, G.L. "Information Technology: A New Competitive Weapon." *Sloan Mangement Review* 25, no. 1 (1983): 3-14.

Porter, Michael E. *Competitive Advantage: Creating and Sustaining Superior Performance*. New York: Macmillan, 1985.

Porter, Michael E. "From Competitive Advantage to Corporate Strategy." *Harvard Business Review* 87, no. 3 (1987): 43-59.

Porter, Michael E. and Victor E. Millar. "How Information Gives Your Competitive Advantage." *Harvard Business Review* 63, no. 4 (1985): 149-160.

[29] Lufthansa, a European airline received the same criticism for its system.

* * *

MANAGING THE ARCHIPELAGO

The "Archipelago of Information Services" is a phrase coined by Warren McFarland and James McKenney in a trilogy of articles that appeared in the *Harvard Business Review* in 1982 and 1983. The phrase Archipelago of Information Services has become a standard phrase to refer to the need to coordinate the activities of different information services and activities, and to refer to the managerial and administrative problems caused by the dispersion of those information activities within different administrative units of the typical business organization.

McFarland and McKenney pointed out various logical historical reasons why the information functions of a typical company are widely dispersed hierarchically. The controllers brought the first computers for accounting purposes and therefore data processing still reports to the chief financial officer; telephone and telecommunications was always considered a general support function and therefore reports to a vice president for administrations; market research was always part of the marketing functions. McFarland and his colleagues argued that these functions could no longer be treated as isolated units. That requirement is driven by the convergence phenomenon, for example the concept that the network is the computer and one can no longer logically or operationally separate computers and telecommunications. That convergence requires some significant degree of common control and coordination of what were here-to-fore separate islands of the archipelago.

Figure 8. Convergence and Integration of the Archipelago

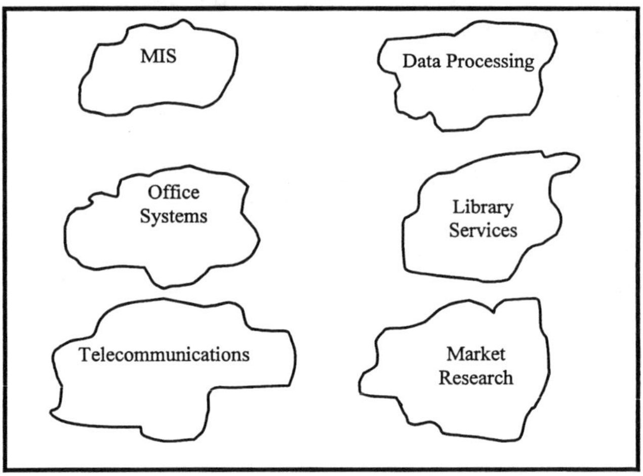

The trilogy of articles points out however that common control and coordination are not easily achieved, precisely because the islands of the archipelago are so scattered and report to so many senior people in the administration. To achieve that common control and coordination requires either a major reorganization of the organization with a great many senior people unhappily relinquishing significant components of their domain, or it requires some sort of horizontal matrix-like coordinating mechanism with the potential risk of inefficiency and excess administrative overhead, or some combination of the above.

Figure 9. Managerial Dispersion of the Archipelago

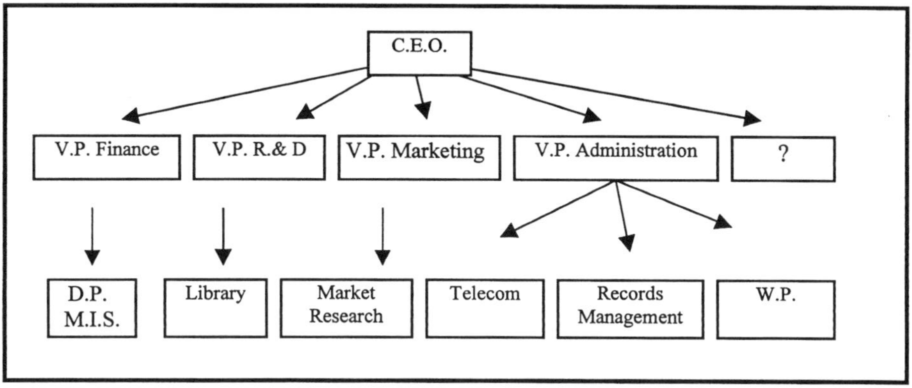

McFarland and McKenney also developed a stage hypothesis, which is really a simplified version of the Nolan stage hypothesis.[30] From it they derive the interesting corollary that different islands in the archipelago will be in different stages of development, and that different stages of information systems development require or at least are best handled by different managerial styles. That is, different islands of the archipelago require different managerial styles, yet they must be coordinated and cannot be treated as islands.

The Archipelago of Information Systems and the Librarian

The shocking news for the librarian is that nowhere in their trilogy do McFarlan and McKenney mention the organization's library as one of the islands in the archipelago. This oversight is galling to librarians. The authors should have included the library for the sake of their own thesis, as often as the corporate library reports to the vice president for research and development since that unit is the heaviest user, and the inclusion of the corporate library would illustrate yet more hierarchical dispersion among the islands of information services.

The positive aspect of the archipelago notion is the emphasis it places on the theme that the coordination of the islands requires top management attention. Since the islands are so scattered, and since they report to such very different parts of the company (see Figure 8), they do not converge administratively or managerially until the apex of the organizational pyramid, the chief executive officer. Only that person can make the organizational changes or establish the control and communication structure necessary to accomplish the coordination and convergence of the islands of the archipelago of information services. This thesis is a very useful complement to the argument that derives from the information technology as competitive advantage theme. Information technology and information handling are too important to be left to the tender ministrations of the divisional chiefs for whom it is merely a support operation, instead it is a matter of critical importance that requires the attention of the chief executive and the top management team. The information technology as competitive advantage thesis makes the argument on the strategic level and the

[30] See the discussion on "Information Systems Stage Hypothesis".

Archipelago of Information Services thesis makes the argument on the tactical and operational level.

Key Articles:

McKenny, James L., and F. Warren McFarlan. "The Information Archipelago Maps and Bridges." *Harvard Business Review* 60, no. 5 (September/October, 1982): 109-114.

McFarlan, F. Warren, James L McKenny, and Philip Pyburn. "The Information Archipelago–Plotting a Course." *Harvard Business Review* 6, no. (January/February, 1983): 145-156.

McFarlan, F. Warren, and James L. McKenny. "The Information Archipelago Governing the New World." *Harvard Business Review* 61, no. 4 (July/August, 1983): 91-99.

* * *

INFORMATION SYSTEMS STAGE HYPOTHESES

In the last two decades, there have been a number of stage theories postulated to help illuminate the typical patterns of growth and development associated with the increasing capability of information technology. In discussion these hypotheses, there is no easy middle course between simply listing them, or describing each of them in sufficient detail to serve as a primer. The latter course, though lengthy, seems clearly preferable.

These hypotheses attempt to derive some order from and more importantly to predict some order in the development of information systems, and thus serve as tools for planning and for management. Given the cost of information technology, and the innate order of an exponential growth such as information technology shows, with no signs of slumping over at some unpredictable point into the standard S shaped logistic growth curve, there is a substantial degree of interest in such hypotheses and a more than average predisposition to expect that they might have some predictive value.

There are two classes of stage hypotheses, the "cyclical" and the "progressive" or developmental. The cyclical or life cycle hypotheses posit that there is a repetitive and predictable life cycle of development as each major new information technology capability comes along, whether that be word processing, or spread sheets, or in-house CD-ROM mastering, or Intranets. Note that the capability may be a hardware development, a software development, or any combination. The second class of stage hypothesis is that of the progressive non-cyclical, non-repetitive hypotheses that try to predict broad-spectrum maturational stages of overall information technology growth.

The Cyclical Stage Hypotheses

Nolan

The first stage hypothesis to gain widespread attention, and probably still the best known, is Nolan's stage hypothesis. Nolan posited that as new information technologies emerge, they had to go through a series of predictable stages. Initially he had four stages in his schema, and he later increased that to six.[31]

Figure 10. Nolan Stage Hypothesis

1. INITIATION	Technology Era
2. CONTAGION	
3. CONTROL	
4. INTEGRATION	
5. DATA ADMINISTRAION	Information Era
6. MATURITY	

Nolan, Richard L. "Managing the Crises in Data Processing." *Harvard Business Review* 57, no. 2 (March/April, 1979): 115-126.

Nolan's schema implies several important corollaries, first a shift in emphasis from the technology to the information being handled, a shift from carrier to content, and second a

[31] R.L. Nolan, "Managing the Crises in data processing," *Harvard Business Review* 57, no. 2 (1979): 115-126.

necessary shift in management style from relatively loose and laissez-faire where experimentation and creativity are encouraged, at the initiation and contagion stages, to a more structured and controlling climate in the subsequent stages.

McFarlan
McFarlan recast the Nolan schema into four stages that place greater emphasis upon the management styles appropriate to each stage. McFarlan's stage hypothesis occurs in the context of analyzing the problems and opportunities that present themselves as organizations face the task of integrating or coordinating the various islands of the archipelago of information units and services.[32]

Figure 11. McFarlan Stage Hypothesis (essentially a recasting of the Nolan Stages)

1. INDENTIFICATION & INITIAL INVESTMENT
2. EXPERIMENTATION & LEARNING
3. CONTROL
4. WIDESPREAD TECHNOLOGY TRANSFER

McFarlan, et al., "The Information Archipelago-Plotting a Course." *Harvard Business Review* 16, no. 1 (Jan.Feb. 1983): 145-156.

These cyclical theories are not uniformly accepted. There have been a number of articles that argue that they are of limited applicability and that they can be misleading if taken too much for granted and applied too simplistically. Nonetheless, these concepts have had a great impact, and Nolan's article is one of the most highly requested that the *Harvard Business Review* has ever published.

The Progressive (Non-cyclical) Stage Hypotheses

These theories or hypotheses apply not to each new technological capability, but to the development over time of information technology as a whole. These schemes try to describe the progression of information technology on a more macro scale, rather like the well known characterization of human development as a series of stages; hunter-gatherer, agricultural, industrial, and post industrial or informational. The information systems stage hypotheses are in fact a schema for sub-stage development within that fourth, post industrial or informational, stage.

Marchand
The first of these stage theories to be broadly promulgated was probably that of Marchand. Based on extensive work in analyzing the use of information systems in government agencies, Marchand postulated a stage hypothesis for the development of integrated

[32] F. W. McFarlan and others "The Information Archipelago-Plotting a Course," *Harvard Business Review* 61, no. 1 (January/February 1983): 145-156.

information management[33], a structure that formed the basis for an extensive body of work by Marchand and Horton.[34]

Figure 12. Marchand Stage Hypothesis

1. PHYSICAL CONTROL
   (1900-1950s)
2. MANAGEMENT OF AUTOMATED TECHNOLOGY
   (1960s – mid 1970s)
3. INFORMATION RESOURCES MANAGEMENT
   (mid 1970s – 1980s)
4. KNOWLEDGE MANAGEMENT
   (late 1980s – 1990s)

Marchand, Donald A. "Strategies and Tools in Transition?" *Business and Economic Review* 20, no. 5 (May 1983): 4-8.

Marchand initially posited four stages (1) Physical Control, (2) Management of Automated Technology, (3) Information Resources Management, and (4) Knowledge Management. Marchand later, in 1986, inserted another stage, business competition analysis and intelligence, between stages 3 and 4.[35]

Rockart

Shortly afterward in 1984, Rockart, who had done extensive systems work in the corporate environment, popularized the argument that information systems were developing through three clearly definable stages: first clerical, second operational, third managerial.[36] Rockart's work, like Marchand's was principally observational rather than either theoretical or grounded in IT capabilities, but it was the basis of the later more detailed work by Gibson and Jackson.

Figure 13. Information Systems Stages (Rockart)

1. CLERICAL
2. OPERATIONAL
3. MANAGERIAL

Rockart, John F., and Scott Morton, Michael. "Implications of Changes in Information Technology for Corporate Strategy." *Interfaces* 14, no. 1 (1984): 84-95.

Koenig

Koenig posited a third progressive stage hypothesis, in 1986. The origin of this stage hypothesis is orthogonal to the others. It derives from a pair of very fundamental

[33] D.A. Marchand, "Strategies and tools in transition?" *Business and Economic Review* 29, no. 5 (1983): 4-8.
[34] D.A. Marchand, and F.W. Horton, *Infotrends: Profiting from Your Information Resources*, New York: Wiley, 1986.
[35] Ibid.
[36] J.F. Rockart and Scott Morton, "Implications of changes in information technology for corporate strategy," *Interfaces* 14, no. 1 (1984): 84-95.

observations: (1) that the doubling periods of the components of information technology tend to become very brief, on the order of a year or two, a phenomenon known as Moores' Law and (2) that there are three fundamental components of information systems: computation, storage, and communication. An analysis of those components in terms of their growth rates, argues Koenig, leads neatly to three stages: Stage I (pre-1971) characterized by exponential Moores' Law growth of computational capability, and relative stasis in storage and communication capabilities, Stage II (1971-1989?) characterized by exponential growth of computation and storage, and relative stasis in communication, and Stage III (post 1989?) characterized by exponential growth of all three components. Koenig also adds a fourth stage, when continuous speech recognition will allow users to converse directly to their information system.[37]

In retrospect, the beginning of Stage II is delineated quite distinctly by the appearance of real time online access to large, millions of records, databases. In 1971, the United States National Library of Medicine launched the Medline service, OCLC the Online Computer Library Center (then the Ohio College Library Center) went operational, and so did the NOTIS system of Northwestern University, the first really successful large scale library catalog automation system. Shortly thereafter in 1972, Systems Development Corporation with its Orbit system and Lockheed Corporation with its Dialog system launched commercial online database searching. Stage III, though not quite so crisply delineated in time, seems clearly to have begun with the explosive growth of the Internet, previously Arpanet.

Figure 14. Information Systems Development Stage Hypothesis (Koenig)

Stage	**Exponential Growth of:**	**Stasis in:**	**Date**
I	Computation	Storage Communication	Pre 1971
II	Computation Storage	Communication	1971-1989
III	Computation Storage Communication		1989-
IV	Computation Storage Communication, and Continuous Speech Recognition		?

Koenig, Michael E.D. "The Convergence of Computers and Telecommunications: Information Management Implications," *Information Management Review* 1, no. 3 (September 1986): 23-33.

[37] M.E.D. Koenig, "Entering Stage III. The Convergence of the Stage Hypothesis," *Journal of the American Society*
for Information Science 43, no. 3 (April 1992): 204-207.

Figure 15. Gibson & Jackson Domains (Benefit/Beneficiary Matrix)

Beneficiary / Benefit	Individual	Functional Unit	Organization
Efficiency	Domain II	Domain I	Domain III
Effectiveness	Domain II	Domain I	Domain III
Transformation	Domain III	Domain III	Domain III

Gibson, Cyrus F., Jackson, Barbara Bund. *The Information Imperative: Managing the Impact of Information Technology on Business and People*. Lexington, Mass.: D.C. Health, 1987.

Domain I is described as the automation of traditional back office operations, yielding benefits to the functional unit, at first greater efficiency and then improved effectiveness. This was the era of the mainframe computer. Domain II, which came about with the advent of the minicomputer to be followed shortly by the microcomputer, resulted in greater efficiency and effectiveness, particularly for end-user computing. Now, they maintain we have entered Domain III which could be described as the era of the network or of the Internet and which will be characterized by greater efficiency and effectiveness for the organization, and by the transformation of jobs, functions, and roles at all levels – individual, functional unit, and organizational.

Zachman

In 1991, Zachman posited a three-stage process for the development of systems software.[38] Zachman posits a general similarity in the design of any sophisticated and complex product, whether that product is airframes or software. For most of his career Zachman was a consultant to the aerospace industry for IBM. In the first stage of the development of complex products, let us say airframes or software, these products are constructed as custom-built, one-of-a-kind implementations. Pushed by consumers, who demand both volume and economy, Stage 1 gives way to Stage 2, mass production of airframes and software. Customer demand is still not satisfied; customers want the benefit of mass production, yet they also want individually configured products. The results is Stage 3, that of "assemble to order" airframes and software.

Zachman argues that while airframe manufacture entered into Stage 3 in the 1960s, software is still primarily in Stage 2, with major vestiges of Stage 1 remaining, and is only now beginning to move into Stage 3, "assemble to order". The ramifications of Stage 3 are extensive and fascinating. One conclusion is that, not only must there be standardization at the level of software interconnection, the seven layer OSI model for example, but even more

[38] Ibid.

importantly there must also be standardization at the level of data and information structuring. Except in a few specialized areas such as bibliographic information, and EDI (Electronic Data Interchange) for product purchases, this is an undertaking that we have only begun to address.

One can also see a connection between the Zachman stage hypothesis and the Nolan stage hypothesis. The Nolan stage hypothesis predicts a shift in emphasis from the technology to the data, from the carrier to the contents. The Zachman stage hypothesis arrives at that same corollary, implying a transition from the standardization of the technology, the carrier, in this case the software, to the standardization of the content, data, and information structure.

Figure 16. Zachman Stage Hypothesis

1 CUSTOM SOFTWARE
2 OFF THE SHELF SOFTWARE
3 ASSEMBLE TO ORDER SOFTWARE

Zachman, John A. Personal Communication, April 1991.

Convergence of the Progressive Stage Hypotheses

Perhaps the most salient and the most fascinating characteristic of the progressive stage hypotheses is the consistency of their view of where we are in the chronology of information systems development. In a reverse of the blind men and the elephant parable, they originate from very different sectors of the information world, take different routes along the way, and yet they all arrive at the same conclusion. If we lay the progressive stage hypothesis out side by side we arrive at the tableau below. (See Figure 17.)

Figure 17. Comparison of Developmental Stage Hypothesis for Information Management

Marchand Stages (1983	Rockart Eras (1984)	Gibson/Jackson Domains (1987)	Koenig Stages (1985)	Zachman Stages (1990)
Stage 1 Management of Automated Technology	First Era Clerical and Accounting	First Domain Efficiency and Effectiveness of Unit Operations	Stage I Exponential Growth of Computation, Stasis in Storage & Communication	Stage I Custom Software
Stage 2 Information Resources Management	Second Era Operational	Second Domain Efficiency and Effectiveness of Individual Operations	Stage II Exponential Growth of Computation & Storage, Stasis in Communication	Stage II Off the Shelf Software
Stage 3	Third Era	Third Domain	Stage III	Stage III
Knowledge Management	Managerial	Efficiency and Effectiveness of the Organization & Transformation	Exponential Growth of Computation & Storage & Communication	Assemble to Order Software
			Stage IV Exponential Growth of Computation & Storage & Communication plus Continuous Speech Recognition	

TIME

(—— = Roughly the present time)

The only modification necessary to fit the stage hypothesis into the comparison table is with Marchand's stage I, "Physical Control" which is treated as out of scope, as it is before the era of automated information systems. One might say that subsequent stage hypothesis implicitly treated that stage as stage 0. Second, Marchand's earlier formulation of his stages is used rather than his later one, on the grounds that the inserted stage, business competition analysis and intelligence, is more of an ongoing parallel function than it is a discrete stage, a view that Marchand himself is not uncomfortable with.[39] While convergence is by no means proof, the degree of convergence in the conclusion, that is that in the 1990s information technology is embarking on a dramatically new stage is both striking and offers a high degree of confidence that the conclusion is not mere happenstance.

The most recent stage hypothesis, by Koenig and Sione, arises from a comparison of the development of net technology, the Internet, with that of previous general enabling technologies.[40] This hypothesis proposes that there is a recognizable and predictable life cycle to important general enabling technologies such as the railroad, or the telephone, or the "Net". This life cycle, in simple terms, consists of three stages.

First, the technology is introduced, experimented with, and developed in a relatively laissez-faire fashion. Second, the technology is recognized as being not just a new toy or a luxury, but something of great importance, even fundamental importance, to society. Societal concerns emerge as to how to provide broad, fair, and equitable access to this new technology. This, in turn, requires the establishment of some sort of structure and concomitant regulation, to ensure equity and access. Third, as the technology becomes near pervasive and societal consensus has emerged as to how to provide that fair and equitable access, then the emphasis can and does shift back to promoting greater competition among providers to thereby enhance efficiency and effectiveness, and the bywords become competition and deregulation. These life cycle stages are most clearly seen in telecommunications, particularly telephony, and in commercial aviation.

The same cycles can be seen however, though somewhat less pronouncedly, in railroads, and in the dynamo and the grid, the system for the distribution of power. If one sketches the phase development of these technologies in the 19th and 20th centuries, it looks like the following graph.

[39] D.A. Marchand, Personal Communication. March, 1988.

[40] M.E.D. Koenig, and P. Sione, "The World at Stage III, but the Net at Stage II." *Journal of the American Society for Information Science* 48, no. 9 (October, 1997): 853-859.

Figure 18. Life Cycles of Major General Enabling Technologies

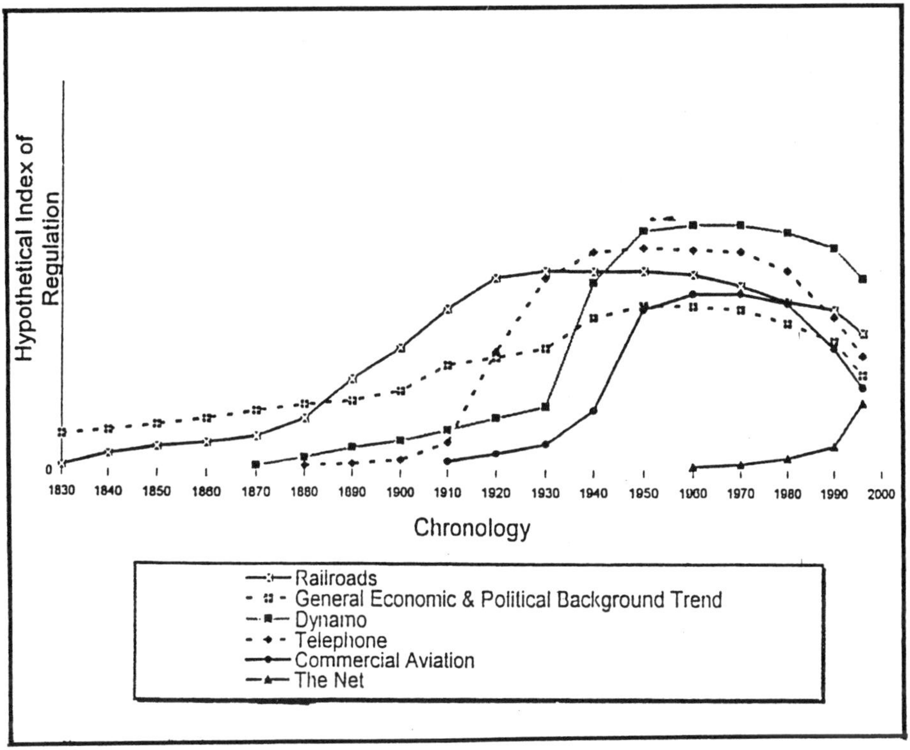

What is striking is that of all the previous great evolving technologies, each following the same general life cycle, some starting in the 19th century, some starting in the 20th century, some following their life cycles more rapidly than others, have all, more or less, coincidentally entered the third stage, the deregulatory stage, of their life cycle at roughly the same time, the last quarter of the 20th century. The consequence of this convergence of third stage technologies now arriving at Stage III, the deregulatory stage of their life cycles, and has come to assume that this is a generic society-wide phenomenon, almost a general stage of societal or economic development.

But, the Net is not entering Stage III, it is just starting Stage II, societal concern about fair and equitable access, the stage that requires structure and regulation. The thesis here then is that the industrial age is at Stage III, but the Net is at Stage II, and there is a fundamental disconnect. Our society perceives itself to be in a generic Stage III, and yet it is becoming aware, if only in a pre-conscious knee-jerk and not clearly articulated fashion, that as far as the network age goes, we are in a quite different stage. The more important the net becomes, the more of an issue the disconnect becomes. The consequence is that the emergence of the need will require society to do substantial rethinking of values and policies.

Stage Hypotheses and the Librarian

The utility of stage hypotheses is to provide a framework that allows for crisper analysis and better planning. The overall thrust of these hypotheses is to argue that we librarians are in the midst of the changes that are molding society. Knowledge of these hypotheses can be used both to substantiate the importance of information technology and information, and the importance of our role. Ideally we can use them to help in guiding our organizations to plan for their future.

Note: See the section on "Knowledge Management and Intellectual Capital" for a brief discussion of another stage representation of the development of knowledge management.

Key Articles:

Gibson, Cyrus F., and Barbara Bund Jackson. *The Information Imperative: Managing the Impact of Information Technology on Business and People*. Lexington, Mass: D.C. Heath, 1987.

Koenig, M.E.D. "Entering Stage III – The Convergence of the Stage Hypotheses." *Journal of the American Society for Information Science* 43, no. 3 (April 1992): 204-207.

Koenig, M.E.D., and P. Sione. "The World at Stage III, but the Net at Stage II." *Journal of the American Society for Information Science* 48, no. 9 (October 1997): 853-859.

Marchand, D.A. "Strategies and Tools in Transition?" *Business and Economic Review* 29, no. 5 (1983): 4-8.

Marchand, D.A., and F.W. Horton. *Infotrends: Profiting from Your Information Resources*. New York: Wiley, 1986.

McFarlan, F.W., J.L. McKenney, and P. Pyburn. "The Information Archipelago Plotting a Course." *Harvard Business Review* 61, no. 1 (1983): 145-156.

Nolan, Richard L. "Managing the Crises in Data Processing." *Harvard Business Review* 57, no. 2 (March/April, 1979): 115-126.

Rockart, J.F., and M. Scott Morton. "Implications of Changes in Information Technology for Corporate Strategy." *Interfaces* 14, no. 1 (1984): 84-95.

*

DECISION ANALYSIS & EVPI, The EXPECTED VALUE of PERFECT INFORMATION

The term decision analysis was coined by the Rand Corporation to describe a methodology for calculating the tradeoff between making a decision with partial information versus expending resources to obtain more information and thereby making a decision based on more complete information. The Rand Corporation is a contract research organization in the United States, noted for doing research on strategic issues for the United States Air Force. The general technique they referred to as decision analysis, and the added value obtained by making a decision based on better information they referred to as the expected value of perfect information (EVPI).

The phrase EVPI is in fact a bit misleading, the obvious point being that one seldom has perfect information. What the technique does is to attempt to calculate the expected negative consequences, the dis-benefit, of making a decision based on less than perfect information, and then calculate how much that dis-benefit would be reduced if the decision could be based on better information, and whether that reduction of dis-benefit is greater than the cost of obtaining that better information. If that reduction of dis-benefit is greater than the cost of obtaining the information, and if time permits, then clearly the appropriate course of action is to spend the resources to get that better information. That alternative of gathering more information is the salient point articulated by decision analysis. Making a decision is in principle it is argued, a cyclical process, and at decision time, an alternative that is always in play is to recycle, gather more and better information, and return to the decision point (see *Figure 19*).

The process of calculating the EVPI, the dis-benefit of making a decision based on less than perfect information, is complex and applicable only in a few situations. The principle is relatively straightforward, the difficulty arises in estimating first the degree of uncertainty attached to different alternatives, and secondly the degree to which those uncertainties are independent of each other. The reader who would like to pursue the topic is referred to the article by Menke. Neither the librarian nor the organization is likely to use EVPI in the normal course of events, but it remains a conceptual notion.

Figure 19. Decision Analysis

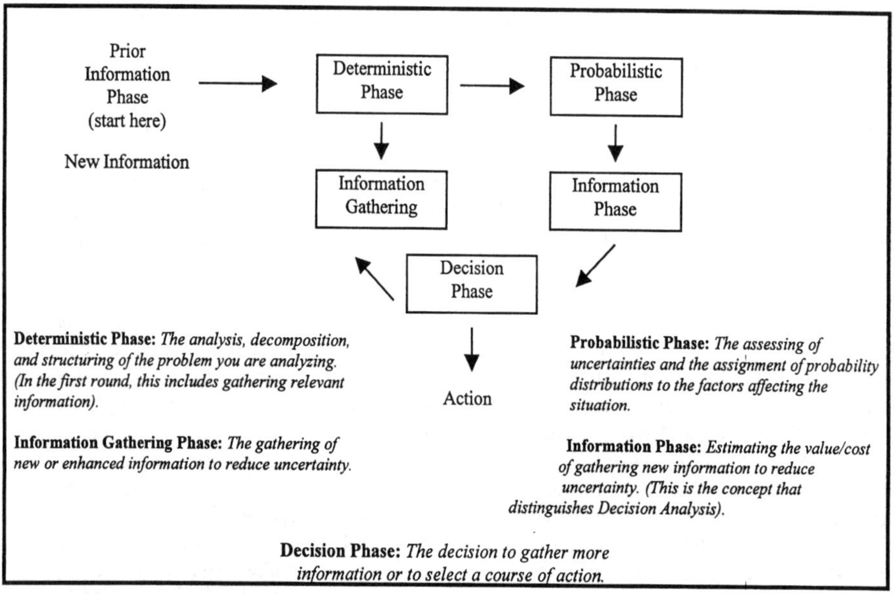

Decision Analysis and the Librarian

What is important about EVPI and decision analysis are two things. First, in a few situations it allows one to place a real value on information, a notoriously difficult commodity to value with any precision. Second and more importantly, it makes the point that there is a cost, the expected dis-benefit, to making a decision based on imperfect information, and that we can reduce that cost by obtaining better information and thereby making a better decision. In only a few highly structured situations, can we calculate those costs, but the principle is an important one for librarians to be able to articulate. At every decision point, there is another alternative, go get better information (and here is when the librarian should be involved) and return to make the decision with an increased likelihood of making the correct decision.

Whenever a major decision is being made, and time permits the possibility of gathering more information the librarian should consider: what better information could be gathered (whether that is a more thorough literature search, hiring consultants, or doing a survey of potential customers for example), what the costs of obtaining that information would be, and consider what uncertainty affects the decision being made, and how the added information would reduce that uncertainty, and be prepared to discuss with senior management the advisability of expending resources to get more and better information before making a decision. Like Enterprise Wide Information Analysis, decision analysis and EVPI highlight the importance of the provision of appropriate information for management decision making.

Key Articles:

Menke, Michael M. "Strategic Planning in an Age of Uncertainty." *Long Range Planning* 12, no. 4 (1979): 27-34.

*

DATA DRIVEN SYSTEMS DESIGN

The importance of data driven systems design is that not the process, not the precise steps to be undertaken, but the information and its flow within the system is the driving factor behind systems design. The origin of this realization lies with what is called "structured Programming". As information systems became larger, frequently with hundreds of thousands of lines of code, two major problems emerged, how could such a system be parceled out to various people for development? How could programmers subsequently find their way back into the dense mass of code to the right spot to make corrections or enhancements? The idea of structured programming was to make the code structured and manageable.

Structured programming developed three major precepts.

1. Document. In particular the precept was that the programmer should exercise the discipline of documenting as they wrote code, interspersing lines of code and lines of textual explanation, and not wait until afterwards to do their documentation. If the programmer waited until afterwards, too often the documentation never got done, and it was often not the programmer's fault, rather the programmer would often be diverted onto another project and the task of documentation would never be returned to.

2. Avoid Go-To Statements. This meant avoiding "spaghetti code" or "go to" statements that took the logic from one place in the code to another distant point. In so far as practical, branching should be kept local, using the "if, then, else" structure of the code locally.

3. Modularize. Break the code into small easily recognized and named chunks.

The last notion, modularization, was probably the most important. Not only does it make it easier to navigate the program after it is written, but it is mandatory for assigning tasks to different development programmers. One can't simply assign the first programmer to write the first ten thousand lines of code, then second the next ten thousand, and so on. One can in principle assign one person to write the serials module or chunk, another the circulation module, another the catalog/user interface module. However, the user at the catalog will want to know not only that the item is in the collection, but also its circulation status. Is it available for loan? Is it on reserve? Is it loaned out, and if so can it be recalled?

In other words, before work on the chunks is undertaken, the needed communication of information between them must be analyzed. The technique that resulted is called data flow analysis, and it basically is very simple. One simply charts the information flow in the organization, starting at the most general and working down to finer and finer levels of granularity. There are only four symbols to use in data flow analysis:

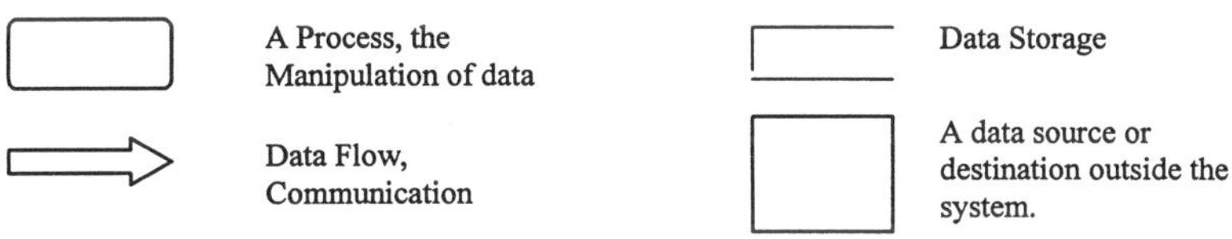

Note that this is very different from traditional logical flow charting, where the ◇ symbol is the equivalent of the "if, then, else" statement, the branching operation of the actual code written.

The whole point of data driven systems design is that before one begins traditional flow charting, one does a data flow analysis of the proposed system. That data flow analysis reveals the logical chunks, the modules of the system and the data, and the information that flows between them. With those chunks and those data flows, one can then assign the chunks, develop traditional logical flow charts for the chunks, design the data stores and then write code.

Data Driven System Design and the Librarian

There are two major points for the librarian. First, the notion of data driven systems design makes unambiguously clear that information systems, that is all data processing systems, are first and foremost <u>information</u> systems. The information and its flow are more fundamental in systems design than is the process. This is a point that all librarians should realize, and about which they should be prepared to remind both management and data processing specialists. After all, we are the information specialists.

The second point is that data flow analysis that is, high level systems design, does not require programming expertise, it requires a knowledge of what the organization does and how information flows in it, and it requires common sense and good analytical skills. Librarians through the nature of their work acquire a broad knowledge of the organization and how it operates, and they frequently possess good analytical skills. There is then an overlap between high level systems design and librarianship that is often unrecognized and that some librarians may wish to the advantage of. For those who are interested in pursuing this topic further, the books by Gane and Sarson, and DeMarco are the standards. This author prefers the presentation by Gane and Sarson and finds their notation more congenial.

Key Articles:

Brookes, Frederick P. Jr. *The Mythical Man Month: Essays on Software Engineering*. Reading, Mass.: Addison Wesley, 1975.

Dahl, O., E. Djikstra, and C. Hoare. *Structured Programming*. New York: Academic Press, 1972.

DeMarco, Tom. *Structured Analysis and System Specification*. Englewood Cliffs, NJ: Prentice Hall, 1979.

Djikstra, E.W. “Go To Statement Considered Harmful.” *Communications of the ACM* 11, no. 3 (1968): 147-149.

Gane, Chris and Trish Sarson. *Structured Systems Analysis: Tools and Techniques*. Englewood Cliffs, NJ: Prentice Hall, 1979.

Martin, James and Carma McClure. *Diagramming Techniques for Analysis and Programmers*. Englewood Cliffs, NJ: 1985.

Yourdon, E. and L.L. Constantine. *Structured Design*. Englewood Cliffs, NJ: Prentice Hall, 1979.

Yourdon, E. *Techniques of Program Structure and Design*. Englewood Cliffs, NJ: Prentice Hall, 1975.

Weinburg, V. *Structure Analysis*. Englewood Cliffs, NJ: Prentice Hall, 1980.

Whitehouse, G.E. *Systems Analysis and Design Using Structured Techniques*. Englewood Cliffs, NJ: Prentice Hall, 1980.

MACRO THEMES & END NOTE

In examining these twenty-one concepts and themes, several macro themes can be seen to run through them. These macro themes have their own utility, either as points that librarians may wish to make, or as providing lessons to be profited from.

1) ***Information Management is Important and Demands Top Management Attention and Involvement.***
   This is a key element in the following themes (in rough order with the degree to which they support this macro theme):
   Knowledge Management and Intellectual Capital
   Information Technology as Competitive Advantage
   Information Technology and Productivity
   Enterprise-Wide Information Analysis
   Managing the Archipelago
   Information System Stage Hypotheses
   Information Technology and Organizational Structure
   Enterprise Resource Planning
   Business Process Reengineering
   Supply Chain Management
   Core Competencies
   Minimization of Unallocated Cost
   Information Resources Management
   TQM and Benchmarking
   and

to at least some degree all of the other themes. The obvious point here, is that information, the commodity in which we deal, and information management, the skills we employ, are important, and are becoming increasingly so.

2) ***As Information Systems Mature, the Emphasis Shifts from the T, Technology, to the I, Information.***
   This perception surfaces frequently in a number of themes:
   Knowledge Management
   Information Systems Stage Hypotheses (particularly the Nolan stage hypothesis, but also Marchand, Koenig, and Zachman)
   Information Driven Marketing
   Information Resource Management
   Enterprise-Wide Information Analysis
   MIS to DSS, and External Information
   Data Driven Systems Design.
   Supply Chain Management

The relevance here is the corollary argument that as information systems mature, the relative importance of information technologists diminishes, while the relative importance of those who know how to manipulate and manage the information itself increases.

3) ***External Information – the Librarian's Domain- is Important and its Importance is often Overlooked.***
This theme, emerges sometimes explicitly as in MIS to DSS, but more often implicitly. The key themes are:
MIS to DSS, and External Information
Competitive Intelligence
Information Driven Marketing
Enterprise-Wide Information Analysis
Data Warehousing / Data Mining
Decision Analysis
Knowledge Management.

This theme is important to librarians. Note however, that much of the important information external to the organization is tacit informal information, an area where we are not perceived to have a great deal to contribute. Use this theme, but use it carefully.

4) ***Releasing the Shackles of Print-on-Paper Technology.***
To some degree, all of the topics share this theme. It is particularly prominent (though seldom explicitly recognized) in:
Business Process Reengineering
Enterprise Resource Planning
Information Technology and Organizational Structure
Information Technology and Productivity
Knowledge Management
Hierarchies to Markets
Data Driven Systems Design
Information Systems Stage Hypotheses (particularly Koenig, and Gibson & Jackson).
Supply Chain Management
The lesson here is that librarians must be careful not to be perceived as wedded or to closely tied to print-on-paper technology, a real danger. Instead, librarians must be perceived as technological au currant, and indeed as actively implementing and embracing change.

The even more important utility of these main themes is that they weave the twenty-one themes and concepts into a structured whole, and help us to grasp and comprehend and visualize that whole. The relationship among the themes and concepts and the Macro Themes can be sketched as a classificatory tree structure, but it is the typical messy tree, with densely interwoven, with one fruit often attached to many branches. (See the following schematic.)

The salient point of this tree is that these twenty-one themes and concepts are not just a shopping list, but they represent a densely interwoven and much larger and very important whole, the notion of information driven management. To close with a theme stressed in the introduction, the librarian may well be in the best position of anyone in the organization to grasp the scope and totality of the larger structure. Thus situated, the librarian is in a position to be not simply a contributor to and implementor of important developments within the organization, but an educator and a change agent with great impact within the organization.

INFORMATION DRIVEN MANAGEMENT THEMES

A Classificatory Structure

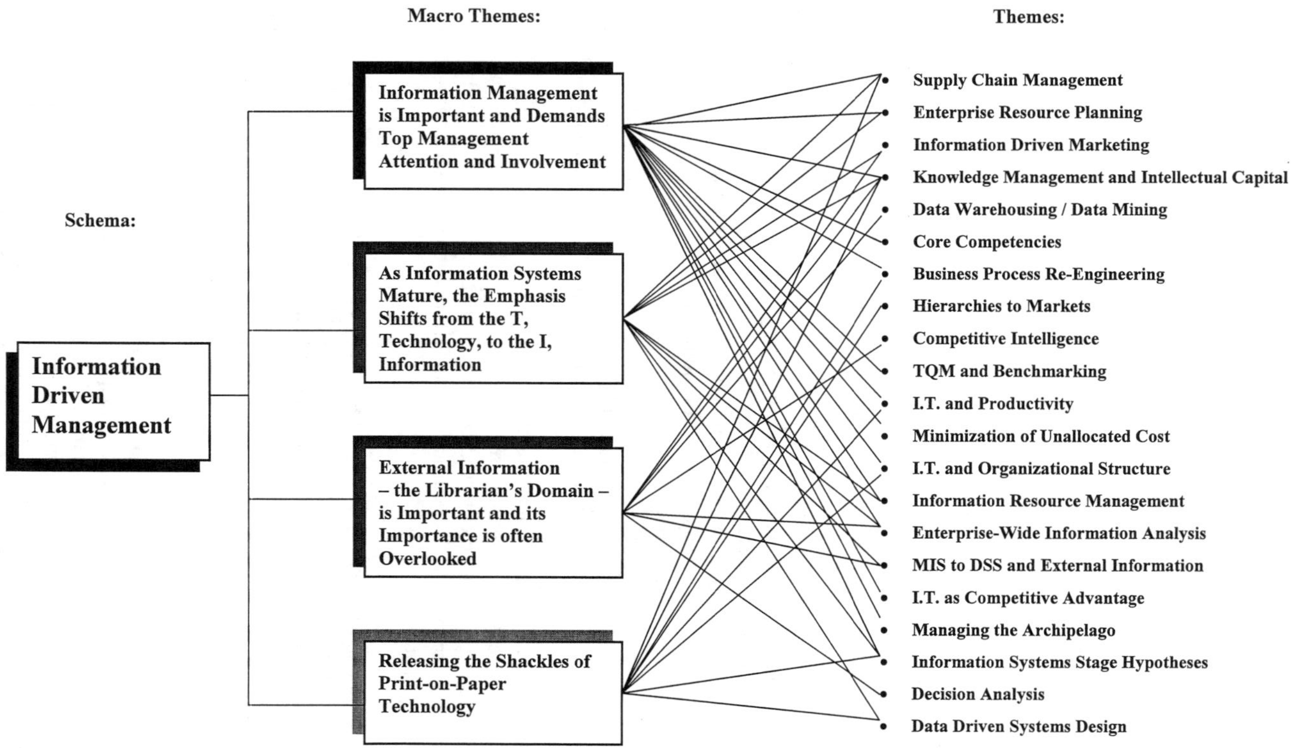

Note to some degree almost every theme can be limited to the Macro Themes of "Information Management is Important…" and "Releasing the Shackles…". The author has tried to select those where the link is particularly germane.

The salient point of this tree is that these twenty-one themes and concepts are not just a shopping list, but they represent a densely interwoven and much larger and very important whole, the notion of information driven management. To close with a theme stressed in the introduction, the librarian may well be in the best position of anyone in the organization to grasp the scope and totality of the larger structure. Thus situated, the librarian is in a position to be not simply a contributor to and implementor of important developments within the organization, but an educator and a change agent with great impact within the organization.